Dramatizing the Political: Deleuze and Guattari

Also by Iain MacKenzie

POLITICS: Key Concepts in Philosophy

THE IDEA OF PURE CRITIQUE

THE EDINBURGH COMPANION TO POSTSTRUCTURALISM (*co-edited with Robert Porter and Benoît Dillet, forthcoming*)

Also by Robert Porter

IDEOLOGY: Contemporary Social, Political and Cultural Theory

DELEUZE AND GUATTARI: Aesthetics and Politics

THE EDINBURGH COMPANION TO POSTSTRUCTURALISM (*co-edited with Iain Mackenzie and Benoît Dillet, forthcoming*)

Dramatizing the Political: Deleuze and Guattari

Iain MacKenzie
University of Kent, UK

and

Robert Porter
University of Ulster, UK

First published 2011 by
PALGRAVE MACMILLAN

Palgrave Macmillan in the UK is an imprint of Macmillan Publishers Limited, registered in England, company number 785998, of Houndmills, Basingstoke, Hampshire RG21 6XS.

Palgrave Macmillan in the US is a division of St Martin's Press LLC, 175 Fifth Avenue, New York, NY 10010.

Palgrave Macmillan is the global academic imprint of the above companies and has companies and representatives throughout the world.

Palgrave® and Macmillan® are registered trademarks in the United States, the United Kingdom, Europe and other countries.

ISBN 978–0–230–58071–8

This book is printed on paper suitable for recycling and made from fully managed and sustained forest sources. Logging, pulping and manufacturing processes are expected to conform to the environmental regulations of the country of origin.

A catalogue record for this book is available from the British Library.

Library of Congress Cataloging-in-Publication Data

Mackenzie, Iain M.
    Dramatizing the political : Deleuze and Guattari / Iain MacKenzie, Robert Porter.
        p. cm.
    Includes index.
    ISBN 978–0–230–58071–8 (hardback)
    1. Deleuze, Gilles, 1925–1995 – Political and social views. 2. Guattari, Félix, 1930–1992 – Political and social views. 3. Political science – Philosophy. 4. Aesthetics – Political aspects. I. Porter, Robert, 1972– II. Title.

JC261.D39M33 2011
320.01—dc23   2011030615

10 9 8 7 6 5 4 3 2 1
20 19 18 17 16 15 14 13 12 11

Printed and bound in Great Britain by
CPI Antony Rowe, Chippenham and Eastbourne

Contents

Acknowledgements

We are grateful to editors and publishers for permission to use revised versions of the following material: 'Dramatization as Method in Political Theory', *Contemporary Political Theory* (forthcoming); 'The Problem with Dramatic Events', *MonoKL* (forthcoming). We are also grateful to have had a number of opportunities to present our developing ideas at conferences and symposia such as: *The Political Studies Association Annual Conference*, 2009; *Schizoanalysis and Visual Culture*, June 2010; *Dramatizing the Political*, September 2009 and 2010. Thanks in particular to Ben Arditi and Ian Buchanan for their kind invitations, and, more generally, to all those who engaged so productively with us at these events.

In a collaborative work of this kind many debts are accrued. We would like to thank everyone who has engaged us in conversation about this project or otherwise helped us bring it to fruition, including Benoît Dillet, George Sotiropoulos, Susan Fitzpatrick, Blaise Verrier, Lewis Kerfane, Anaïs Lasvigne, Daniel Jewesbury, Steve Baker, Ciara Chambers, Martin McLoone, Maire Messenger-Davies and Phil Ramsey. We would especially like to thank Benoît Dillet for his close reading of the text and for his sterling work in compiling the index. Robert would also like to express his gratitude to University of Ulster for invaluable and timely study leave in Autumn/Winter 2010/11.

Without the love and support of our families this book would not have been possible and it is dedicated to them: Kerry-Ann, Jessica, Anna, Kathryn, Sam and Anna.

Introduction

The Zapatistas, a revolutionary group based in the Chiapas region of Mexico, only ever appear in public masked. When asked why they will say, 'We hide our faces so that we may be seen'. For the Zapatistas, their masks represent the politically invisible nature of some of Mexico's poorest people. It is a statement about the failure of the Mexican political system to recognize part of its own population as legitimate members of 'the Mexican people' the system claims to represent (Evans, 2010). By hiding their faces the Zapatistas are proclaiming their exclusion from the political domain – hiding behind masks in order to make visible their invisibility. It is a dramatic technique that reaches back to the beginnings of drama: masking the face precisely to make certain features more visible by excluding others, and to highlight the dynamics between characters by enhancing the forces at work within their emotional, social and political interactions. Indeed, the use of dramatic techniques to intensify political causes has a long history: it would not be too much of an exaggeration to say that every significant revolutionary movement, in the broadest sense of that term, has had its dramatic elements. As well as masks, we can think of the costumes adopted by political movements, the flags people have rallied around, the routines of behaviour that characterize marches and demonstrations, the revolutionary songs adopted by radicals of various sorts, the toppling of sculptures, the use of city squares as platforms on which rebellions are staged, and much else besides. These dramatic elements heighten and intensify the issues at stake: they bring to life spaces within the political domain that were thought dead; they bring into existence new political characters; they stage new forms of the political rather than presuming that it is a domain already defined by the activities of traditional, everyday politics. There is good reason to think that when the political is at stake, when everyday politics no longer enables people to have their say or make their presence felt, an integral part of the challenge will be the use people make of some elements of dramatic form. The dramatization of struggle would seem to be intrinsic to any struggle itself.

In this book we will examine a particular link between dramatization and articulations of the political: the method of dramatization that animates the work of Gilles Deleuze and Félix Guattari. It will be argued, by way of an in-depth engagement with this method as it appears throughout their work, that in order to know the political, political theorists must change it – dramatically. This deliberate echo of Marx's famous thesis eleven (McLellan, 2000, 173) draws out a further claim that will guide our investigation: dramatization is a critical method. By this we mean that there is no Archimedean perspective that this method provides that enables distanced contemplation of our political situation in a manner that separates our knowledge of the political from our political commitments. Alongside other critical methods, it is central to the idea of dramatization that the political world can only be known by way of an explicitly critical intervention. Dramatization, as we will show, adds the claim that this intervention must take a dramatic – by which we mean a practical, critical and creative – form. This is the main theme of Part One.

As with other critical methods, however, once this link between epistemology and critical practice is forged, our understanding of how this method should be deployed must also change. In our case, what we do as political theorists must change if we can only know the political by way of a dramatic intervention in everyday political life. The change is twofold: on the one hand, we must acknowledge that the political can be accessed by looking beyond the world of institutional and party politics; on the other hand, we must avoid an imperial attitude to the broader world of the political and approach it in ways that seek to learn how it is expressed through forms other than traditional political institutions. Put like this, however, it is equally clear that dramatic interventions are not the sole preserve of 'paid-up' political theorists. Rather, if we think of the project of political theory as the articulation of the political, then this project is always already underway across a whole array of personal, cultural, social, sexual, economic and political forms (to name a few). We will explore some of these forms and the complexities to which they give rise as we put the method of dramatization to work through an analysis of language, the cinematic image and events in Part Two.

Drawing these threads together, the dramatization of the political can be understood as a new way of thinking about *how* the concepts of political theory express the idea of the political (as an alternative approach to the traditional activity of political theorists), *where* dramatic conceptualization takes place (thereby broadening the scope of political theory beyond preoccupations with institutions and norms) and *who*, and/or *what*, thinks the political (so as to allow the possibility that 'the theorist' may be a film or a crowd as well as an individual in an academic institution). These different facets are joined together by the idea that to dramatize the political, in the manner of Deleuze and Guattari, is to make a work of art. The dramatization of the political, therefore, forges a methodological link between politics and aesthetics. As we will argue, dramatization expresses the intrinsically aesthetic nature of moments of politicization – those moments when the machinations of politics are deemed insufficient to meet the demand of the political – and it does so by way of constructing an aesthetic response to those moments. The proper methodological response to a significant political event, for example, is to treat it as an art-work that demands a response appropriate to its form – that is, another work of art. This claim serves as the guiding provocation that runs through the book. Explaining its many features and dealing with the many complexities to which it gives rise anchors the various interpretations and discussions as we progress throughout.

To this end, we will be challenging the normative mainstream within political theory that typically situates political criticism within the terrain of moral philosophy as well as the predominant agonistic challenge to that mainstream that tends to prioritize the category of the social as the ground of the political. In both cases, the political is already defined, despite protestations to the contrary, by virtue of it being subsumed within an already structured domain: the moral in the first case and the social in the second. That said, it would appear that our claim regarding the intrinsically artistic nature of political method falls into the very same trap: perhaps we are subsuming the political within the aesthetic. It is a problem that will come increasingly into focus as we move through the book. As we formulate it, the problem is that of modernism and the conflicting desires it involves: on the one hand, the desire to appropriate non-philosophical domains into the service of philosophical argument; on the other hand, the desire to claim, by way of that appropriation, that art (in particular) is an autonomous form abstracted from its material conditions. To what extent can the method of dramatization be said to have overcome this modernist tension? We will argue that this tension can be overcome if we reconsider the relationship between philosophy and art as described by Deleuze and

Guattari (in *What is Philosophy?*) and if we are careful to treat language as an artistic medium that can pass directly into sensation, as an artwork does. In this sense, dramatizing the political is not simply a critical method vis-à-vis other forms of political thought but a way of doing political philosophy that explicitly links it to the need to challenge the institutions and formations of everyday politics by way of an art of critical intervention – through writing, but also cinema and other image-forms, as well as the dramatic irruptions of political movements.

The many complications and tensions implied in these opening remarks will be addressed, expanded upon, clarified and (for the most part) resolved in the chapters that follow. Recognizing that the whole-scale challenge we mount with respect to many of the guiding presuppositions of political theory may appear outlandish when stated as baldly as they have been above, it is our aim to take the reader on a journey towards these conclusions that begins on much more familiar territory. In the first chapter, therefore, Deleuze and Guattari's contribution to political theory is introduced by way of a discussion of liberty and as a critical perspective on the social-theoretical grounds of contemporary deliberative theory – namely Habermas's theory of communicative action. Both contributions make it clear that Deleuze and Guattari have much to offer political theory, even when that offer is understood as bringing their work alongside dominant concepts and paradigms, in the form of a montage. That said, we close the first chapter by claiming that their contributions will remain partial and insufficiently understood if we do not grasp the methodological apparatus animating their treatment of political concepts. It is not simply that Deleuze and Guattari have a contribution to make to political theory as we usually understand it; rather, they have a new way of thinking about how we understand the nature of what we do as political theorists.

The aim of chapter two, therefore, is to elaborate upon the idea that their contribution is at the level of method. It will be argued that dramatization can be situated within a lineage of critical methods that stem from Marx's thesis eleven – a lineage that accepts that the political world can only be known through the activity of changing it. In this sense, dramatization can be situated on the established terrain of methods in political theory, albeit at the outer reaches of that terrain. Moving beyond the claim that it has a place to occupy in the method debates, it is important to specify dramatization with a view to articulating its core features. The first part of this task is carried out in the remainder of chapter two as we discuss the complex formation and mutation of dramatization within the single-authored work of Deleuze and the jointly authored work of Deleuze and Guattari. We will argue that Deleuze understood dramatization as a practical, critical and creative method for the determination of concepts that Guattari then understood as intrinsically political. In making this claim, however, we tell a complex story of how dramatization emerged as a recognizable method in Deleuze, was critiqued (apparently) as his work with Guattari flourished, yet persisted under different names in their joint and later singly authored works. The complexities of this interpretation are not made any simpler by their last work together, *What is Philosophy?* While dramatization does not appear as an explicit methodological motif, it is clear that the form, language and structure of this book is dramatological – not least, in the evocation of conceptual personae. However, beyond this interpretive point, there is a deeper issue at work. *What is Philosophy?* presents an account of philosophy and its relationship to art that both clarifies and obscures the idea of dramatizing the political. It is clarified by virtue of being given a basis in a thoroughly constructivist account of philosophy and art; it is obscured by virtue of the (apparent) separation Deleuze and Guattari create between these disciplines as well as the lack of an overt role for politics in their account. At the end of this chapter we discuss how this tension can be understood as a modernist tension within their work. It leads us to ask: does the method of dramatization imply a series of modernist presuppositions that it was supposed to have overcome?

The first step in answering this question is taken in chapter three. This chapter details the ontological assumptions that underpin dramatization as method. The nature of dramatization as a practical, critical and aesthetic activity, as detailed in the previous chapter, is generalized into a claim about the relationship between concepts and ideas. Dramatization is presented as the method appropriate to the determination of concepts, by which it is meant that the method enables access to the ideas that they express. The first half of the chapter deals with this issue: how concepts can be said to express ideas. But this is only part of the process of dramatization. The dramatization of the political is not simply about determining the nature of political concepts in order to access the idea of the political; it is also about how the idea of the political is transformed by our dramatic conceptualizations. This double movement of dramatization can be thought of as the mutual conditioning of concept and idea. It is a mutual conditioning that is, we argue, crucial to understanding the politics of dramatization as that which takes place beyond the confines of the academy. By this stage, the main features of dramatization as a method in political theory and as a critical and creative method with real political impact have been determined and it is time to move on to how it can be put to work.

The motif of 'putting dramatization to work' drives the second part of the book, but not with the aim of applying that which we have learnt in Part One – which would suggest a problematic separation of the method from its practice – but with a view to addressing the problem of modernism identified in the first part. It is only by deploying the method that the real nature of this problem and the potential solutions to it can be properly articulated. Chapter four begins on relatively familiar territory, developing themes from chapter one with a discussion of Deleuze and Guattari's work on language and linguistics. As with the general discussion of their political theory, indeed, we argue that their contribution can be understood both as a critique of certain forms of contemporary linguistics and that they are dramatists working in the medium of language. Connecting to earlier discussions, we draw out the importance of humour in their work as a form of artistic political intervention. This is generalized into a claim regarding the critical and political function of slogans as speech acts that express the functioning of order-words within language. At the close of this chapter, a particular slogan is addressed – Belfast is a post-conflict city! – in order to show how slogans serve to articulate dramatically the forces at work within the idea of the political they institute. In many respects, however, this discussion of language, through humour and slogans, merely brings the modernist problem in Deleuze and Guattari into sharper relief.

Chapter five frames this problem in its most direct and explicit way, not least because Rancière and Badiou have discussed Deleuze's treatment of cinema in these critical terms. As Rancière argues, Deleuze's work on cinema is committed to the idea that it is revolutions in cinematic form that manifest cinematic artistic autonomy such that Deleuze does not escape 'modernist theory'. In this chapter, therefore, we outline these criticisms and address them in the context of cinema and in the broader context of our understanding of dramatization as artistic method. In particular, Deleuze's analysis of the operation of cliché and money in cinema is developed with a view to analyzing how these concepts function in and through both language about cinema and cinema itself. This enables us to set up the problem of what happens when we dramatize. In other words, the analysis turns to a broader understanding of the modernist problem as a problem regarding dramatic events. This, then, is our key theme in the sixth chapter.

All throughout the book we will emphasize implicitly and explicitly that various aesthetic and cultural forms can dramatize political concepts, that something happens to concepts (they are heightened, intensified, brought into sharper relief) to the extent that they are dramatized as such. And in chapter six we focus specifically on the significance of this notion that 'something happens' – or, as we more technically put it, on the 'problem of dramatic events'. For us, a dramatic event immediately implies the possibility of having some kind of direct experience that has a significance that is intrinsic to the moment of dramatization as it occurs. And yet, we will show that such dramatic events remain problematic by nature. This is where Deleuze (and Guattari) come in, and why it will also become important to cross-compare their philosophy of the event with that of Badiou. What will prove particularly significant for us is the way in which these philosophies of the event immediately put a clear question mark against our intuition that it is possible to directly experience a dramatic event, that there is an intrinsic significance to dramatic events *qua events*. This montage of Badiou's and Deleuze's concepts of the event enables us, towards the end of the chapter six, to reassert, in a more refined form, our claim that it is possible to have a direct experience that has a significance intrinsic to the moment of dramatization as it occurs, that it is possible to experience a dramatic event from within its dramatic or aesthetic unfolding. Indeed, we shall conclude our discussions by working through the suggestion (one that draws strongly on elements of Deleuze and Guattari, and indeed Badiou, but also departs from them in important ways) that dramatic events can be productively described as works of art.

The above introductory sketch of chapters one through six can undoubtedly be read as a provocation. And this is not simply because we have stated rather flatly a number of contestable claims that need to be developed as the chapters unfold below. For the establishment and defence of a Deleuze–Guattarian method of dramatization also immediately carries with it a number of broad implications or provocations, particularly when thought about in relation to the established disciplinary norms of political theory. This, as we indicated earlier, is something we emphasize and speculate about in chapter one. And it is a theme to which we return in the conclusion when we provide three propositions or slogans that, to our minds, help further crystallize some of the important implications that follow from developing the method of dramatization. It is important that these propositions be read as an invitation to put the method of dramatization to further work, as a series of suggestive remarks concerning how and where we see the method developing in the future. In many respects, our concluding remarks to the book (and the book as a totality, of course) are directed to a readership that we have had in mind since the inception of the project (though, we, of course, realize that imagining or targeting audiences is a risky, difficult and rather problematic business). On the one hand, political theorists (and those working more generally within political studies) who engage with the related problems of method and critique and who, for whatever reason, feel unmoved or less than enthusiastic about engaging with the work of Deleuze and Guattari. And, on the other hand, those working with Deleuze–Guattarian concepts across a variety of disciplines (philosophy, cultural and media studies, fine art, linguistics, literary theory and so on) who may feel reluctant to insist on the methodological significance of their work, perhaps viewing methodological questions as inappropriate or incompatible with key aspects of Deleuze and Guattari's thought.

As we have already implied above, the methodological significance of Deleuze and Guattari's work is that it inevitably moves us towards a consideration of the importance of the art-work, or aesthetics more generally. As we argue in our closing remarks to the book, political philosophers need to start thinking like artists or, better still, along with artists, in bringing to life concepts that provoke, resonate and allow us to meaningfully access the domain of the political. It is no accident that during the course of writing this book we both have (in our own singular ways, but in ways that would not have been possible without our collaboration here) begun to engage in various projects and in collaborations with artists and others working outside the particular confines of the discipline of political theory, or indeed the academy as such. The experience of these collaborations (and our own collaboration in writing this book) has led us to the conclusion that the membrane that separates political practices and aesthetic practices is increasingly porous, and that we need to be increasingly open to moving through the emerging spaces in which aesthetic and political practices resonate and connect up.

While we see some inspiring examples of contemporary political philosophers engaging productively in aesthetic practices and collaborations (we mention Simon Critchley explicitly in the conclusion), we still see these – however notable and worthy – as exceptions. If we have a general cultural complaint, it is that art-work or aesthetic practices are often conservatively viewed as being beyond the purview of serious philosophical thought. And often when they are championed, this is done by way of a philosophical appropriation, whereby the art-work becomes merely illustrative window-dressing confined within the frame of a philosophical meta-language that determines and domesticates it in advance. The importance of Deleuze and Guattari's method of dramatization is precisely in its provocation or invitation to take seriously the idea that philosophical-political thought, or the very formulation of political concepts, implies an aesthetic moment, a drama that necessarily and inevitably plays through conceptualization as such. Let us now begin to raise the curtain on this drama.

Part I

1
Deleuze and Guattari and Political Theory

Deleuze and Guattari are political theorists; their philosophy should be read as political philosophy. This claim may seem rather obvious, but it can also be read as a provocation. In many respects, it makes obvious sense to speak of Deleuze and Guattari as political thinkers, and the secondary literature on their political thought is testimony to the rich resources their work provides for scholars working in this field of enquiry (Hardt, 1993; Goodchild, 1996; Kaufman and Heller 1998; Patton, 2000; Braidotti, 2002; Thoburn, 2003; Read, 2003; Buchanan and Thoburn, 2008; Genosko, 2009). As is evident from this literature, Deleuze and Guattari's oeuvre is replete with both important analyses of the core concepts of political thought (the state, ideology, capitalism, power and institutions, merely to name a few) and a richly articulated new lexicon of political concepts (de- and re-territorialization, nomadology and the war-machine, for example). Given this, their place amongst political thought's great conceptual innovators should not be difficult to secure. However, within political theory (we refer here very specifically to English-speaking political theory and to English-speaking political studies more generally) this place can still be characterized as marginal or, better still, precarious. For while the secondary literature on Deleuze and Guattari's work in the English-speaking world since the late 1990s has grown significantly, and while academics across various humanities disciplines and educational institutions have begun to speak their language, it remains the case that, institutionally speaking, Deleuze and Guattari have yet to be fully established as part of the canon of contemporary political theory.

There are undoubtedly many reasons for their current precarious position within political theory. Perhaps the most obvious and most commonly noted, though, is the fact that Deleuze and Guattari have always actively resisted the idea that the political philosophy of capital-ism undertaken in their major joint works *Anti-Oedipus* and *A Thousand Plateaus* should provide readers with any kind of political programme, let alone a readily identifiable policy framework (Buchanan and Thoburn, 2008, 1). Even those most sympathetic to their analysis of capitalist politics have struggled with this desire to avoid political programmes. Consider Deleuze's well-known conversation with Negri, for example, where the latter tentatively suggests to Deleuze that the lack of program-matic direction renders his and Guattari's project hard to follow, that there are 'points where it's not clear where the "war-machine" is going' (Deleuze, 1995, 171). In response, Deleuze is clear that 'political phi-losophy must turn on the analysis of capitalism' (171) but equally that there is no single direction this turn must follow because, as he argues, 'we've no sure way of maintaining becomings, or still more of arousing them, even within ourselves.... There's no longer any image of proletar-ians around of which it's just a matter of becoming conscious' (173). It is true that without this clear sense of a critical or revolutionary agent it is hard to imagine what their political programme might look like. But, in our view, this should not be taken to mean that we must find a programme within their work in order for them to qualify as politi-cal theorists. Rather, to exclude Deleuze and Guattari from contempo-rary political theory on the grounds that they have produced a body of thought that explicitly and self-reflexively resists any easy translation into a relatively clear and cogent political programme is to privilege a certain understanding of what constitutes political theory. As we will argue throughout, it is the manner in which they challenge this domi-nant idea of what constitutes political theory – that it should result in a prescriptive political programme – that constitutes their profound intervention as political philosophers. In other words, it is not so much what Deleuze and Guattari offer to an established idea of political phi-losophy that is important – though they do that to some extent as well – but the way in which they transform our idea of what it is to do politi-cal philosophy. If political thought can be broadly defined as thinking about the nature of the political domain, Deleuze and Guattari provide a new image of thought that changes what we think we are doing as we try to access this domain. It is with this in mind that we will pursue in depth the method of dramatization that drives their conceptual inno-vations but also crucially anchors their transformation of what it means to do political theory.

The elaboration of this method, however, is by no means a straight-forward matter. To the extent that it has been foregrounded within interpretations of their work (Boundas and Olkowski, 1994) it has been done from a philosophical point of view. This has produced, and continues to produce, significant contributions to our understanding of Deleuze and Guattari, but it remains at some distance from the domain of political theory. Our strategy is to foreground political theory and then work towards the philosophical claims that underpin the method they employ (Part One) with the aim of then putting the method to work (Part Two). As such, we intend this discussion to serve as a route into their work for political theorists, but also as a route that will clarify some of the political implications of the more philosophical discussions of their method.

In this chapter we begin this journey by exploring two ways in which their work can be said to contribute to political philosophy; that is, as a contribution to classic debates within normative political philosophy and as a contribution to how we understand the social-theoretical apparatus that sustains dominant forms of normative political thought. With regard to the former, we will follow Patton's (2000) lead in showing how Deleuze and Guattari's work can be constructed as a contribution to one of the mainstays of political theory, the debates spawned by Berlin's analysis of the two concepts of liberty (Berlin, 2002). With regard to the latter, we delve into the social-theoretical foundation of the communicative turn that sustains much cutting-edge work in contemporary political theory, Habermas's theory of communicative action (Habermas, 1984). In the first instance, the aim is to show that Deleuze and Guattari have significant contributions to make at both these levels, and to this extent their work should become a standard point of reference within these debates.

As our aim is to stress the methodological importance of their contribution, however, it is clear that we need to illuminate the form as well as the content of their contribution (to the point where eventually this dichotomy itself will be superseded). In order to approach this dual task gently, so to speak, we will unfold the dramatic elements of their approach through their use in this chapter (before tackling interpretive and systematic ontological issues in chapters two and three). We begin by situating Deleuze and Guattari in a dramatic montage of different conceptions of freedom; by montage we mean the creation of a terrain of inquiry that subtly overlaps different conceptions with a view to showing where Deleuze and Guattari may be sited on that terrain. As developed within film and theatre, montage is a particularly good technique for the establishment of a frame of connections without overlaying these connections with a sense of their necessary continuity. We then consider the nature of this territory or frame itself, and we do so by excavating the presumptions that animate the communicative paradigm outlined by Habermas, arguably the most significant and certainly most widely established frame of reference within contemporary political theory. In dramatic terms, especially those of the theatre, to bring to light this background frame of reference is to reveal the empty space (Brook, 2008) that conditions the performance space. In political theory, analogously, it is to foreground the idea of political theory that conditions what political theorists do when they do political theory. The aim here is to show that Habermas's theory of communicative action does not succeed in articulating this territory because it can only proceed on the basis of an already-ordered domain: the allegedly 'empty space' is already filled by a certain idea of the political. We will conclude by arguing that these two interventions at the normative and social-theoretical heart of contemporary political theory reveal the need to delve more deeply into Deleuze and Guattari's method of dramatization. The challenge of that method is to articulate fully the relationship between the conditions and the activity of political theory – a relationship we will come to argue, by the close of this book, is one that is necessarily and intrinsically aesthetic.

Montage-effect: Deleuze and Guattari as political theorists

It is clear that Patton's writings have, over a number of years, done much to define how one should present Deleuze's (and Deleuze and Guattari's) concepts in a form that is amenable, interesting and meaningful to political theorists of various stripes (see, among others, Patton 2000; 2005; 2007; 2010). Patton's discussion of what he calls 'critical freedom' in Deleuze and Guattari is a typically good example of his pedagogical flair in this respect (2000, 83–87). It is a discussion presented against the backcloth of Berlin's classic defence of 'negative liberty' and Charles Taylor's equally famous critique of the concept (Berlin, 2002; Taylor, 1985b). Drawing on Deleuze and Guattari's *A Thousand Plateaus*, Patton emphasizes the extent to which they rely on an 'ethics of freedom'. Patton recognizes, however, that in order to make the connections to the established debate it is 'necessary to clarify the concept of freedom involved':

> The Deleuzean ethic…of freedom…systematically privileges processes of creative transformation and metamorphosis through which individual and collective bodies may be transformed. Implicit in

this...is a concept of critical freedom, where 'critical' is understood not in the sense that relates to criticism or judgment, but in the technical sense which relates to a crisis or turning point in some process.... Critical freedom differs from the standard liberal concepts of positive and negative freedom by its focus upon the conditions of change or transformation in the subject, and by its indifference to the individual or collective nature of the subject. By contrast, traditional liberal approaches tended to take as given the individual subject and to define freedom in terms of a capacity to act without hindrance in the pursuit of one's ends or in terms of the capacity to satisfy one's most significant desires. (Patton, 2000, 83)

We can clearly see from this passage Patton's direct invitation to political theorists to engage with the provocation of Deleuze and Guattari's political thought as a contribution to conceptual analysis (in this case, of course, the concept of 'freedom'). He deliberately chooses to cross-compare Deleuze and Guattari with established and famous figures from within the canon of political thought in order to situate Deleuze and Guattari's work on a terrain that is familiar. In our view, however, he does so with the aid of a montage that enacts a two-fold manoeuvre: the introduction of Deleuze and Guattari on to a familiar terrain and the simultaneous de-familiarization of that terrain. Let us delve into his argument in a bit more detail to see how this two-fold process operates. We can recall that Berlin famously articulates negative liberty by way of a particular spatial metaphor: it is the 'area of non-interference' (2002, 170). As Patton outlines, this notion of negative liberty entails two intimately related aspects (2000, 83–84). First, there is a relatively static (Deleuze and Guattari would say 'majoritarian') subject with given capacities (an ability to act freely, for example), desires and goals (a will to act freely, where such action becomes, most notably, an end in itself). Second, and this necessarily follows from Berlin's spatial metaphor, the freedom of the subject requires drawing a boundary around the givenness of the subject. For while the boundaries between the subject and some external agent (the tyrant, the state, the law, other individuals and so on) may be drawn and redrawn differently in different political contexts, the space of non-interference itself ought to remain inviolable, normatively speaking.

Taylor's critique of negative liberty puts less emphasis on the subject's inviolability vis-à-vis a threatening external agent, and emphasizes instead the self-realization of a subject capable of 'strong evaluation' (Taylor, 1985a). To engage in strong evaluation, Taylor argues, is to engage in qualitative judgments and interpretations of right and wrong, better and worse, and these judgments are necessarily made against the backcloth of the things that significantly matter to the self in question. That is to say, individuals can act freely to the extent that they are able to develop an interpretively rich and articulate sense of their most significant values. In contrast to the negative conception of liberty as an area of non-interference, this positive conception takes freedom to mean 'self-mastery'; being in control of one's own sense of value. The following passage is a particularly good example (because it is, we would say, a well-dramatized example) of what Taylor means by 'strong evaluation':

> Let us say that at the age of 44 I am tempted to pack up, abandon my job and go to some other quite different job in Nepal. One needs to renew the sources of creativity, I tell myself, one can fall into a deadening routine, go stale, simply go through the motions of teaching the same old courses; this is premature death. Rather rejuvenation is something that one can win by courage and decisive action; one must be ready to make a break, try something totally new…. All this I tell myself when the mood is on me. But then at other moments, this seems like a lot of adolescent nonsense. In fact nothing in life is won without discipline, hanging in, being able to last through the periods of mere slogging until something greater grows out of them. One has to have…standing loyalties to a certain job, a certain community; and the only meaningful life is that which is deepened by carrying through these commitments, living through the dead periods in order to lay foundations for the creative one. (Taylor, 1985a, 26–7)

This picture of 'strong evaluation' so engagingly painted by Taylor very persuasively brings to light the interpretive backcloth without which it is impossible to articulate the meaning or significance of the concept of 'liberty'. Of course, we can talk about liberty in the negative terms that Berlin does, but it is crucial, for Taylor, that we recognize that even this presupposes a background conception of what is significant to us as 'purposive beings' (Taylor, 1985a, 219). To the extent that the concept of negative liberty rests upon detaching us from this background it is, Taylor argues, inconsistent; an argument he later generalizes with regard to all 'atomist' accounts of human nature (Taylor, 1985b, 187–205).

While Taylor's moral ontology of the self, most comprehensively developed in *Sources of the Self* (Taylor, 1989), may be clearly seen as a radical deepening of Berlin's notion of liberty (indeed, a deepening of the

legalism and proceduralism of liberal political philosophy more generally), it still remains, as Patton says, 'tied to a concept of the subject
as a given, determinate structure of interests, goals or desires' (Patton,
2000, 84). In other words, Taylor, like Berlin, is working with a concept
of freedom that takes for granted a bounded subject acting in accordance with his or her significantly defined interests and desires. The
danger here, from a Deleuze–Guattarian perspective at least, is that
these two concepts of freedom, given what they share, may overlook
the subject's potentially transformative capacities. If this is the case
then political theorists may fail to appreciate fully how and why transformations in the subject can be experienced as moments of liberty
(Patton, 2000, 84).

While it would be wrong to say that contemporary liberal political philosophy remains ignorant of, or unconcerned with, the transformation of the subject, and while the notion of a 'critical freedom'
expressed through the subject's critically reflexive attitude to its current constitution or situation may be seen as a liberal concern (it is
worth noting that Patton takes the term 'critical freedom' from Tully,
1995), it is nonetheless important to recognize how this very familiar
tradition of contemporary political thought begins to get de-familiar-
ized as Patton introduces Deleuze and Guattari into the picture. The
familiar terrain and the set of conceptual problems that we associate
with well-established and mainstream liberal political philosophy
(the problem of freedom) is gradually opened out onto Deleuze and
Guattari's conceptual lexicon as Patton concludes his discussion of
freedom by beginning to speak the Deleuze–Guattarian language of
'assemblages', 'becoming', 'event', 'qualitative multiplicity' and so on.
These concepts then take on the resonance of a rather more insistent
and de-familiarizing provocation (we need to think in terms of 'assemblages' rather than 'subjects'; let's think in terms of 'events' rather than
'changing conceptions of the good') that cannot be so easily ignored or
dismissed as being beyond the purview of political theory as we may
more familiarly understand it.

And this is the point that we would like to emphasize in this context. For even if we wanted to take issue with how Patton constructs
this picture (for instance, he underestimates the extent to which Taylor's
moral ontology of the self allows for transformative moments in the subject), the critical pedagogical function of this particular argument about
'critical freedom' is that it has a curious, provocative, de-familiarizing,
montage-effect. We move or cut from Berlin, to Taylor, to Tully, and
then to Deleuze and Guattari. The montage-effect of setting Deleuze

and Guattari alongside well-established figures and debates in political thought, of making their unfamiliar and provocative concepts resonate through a set of conceptual problems already familiar to political theorists, is not just helpful commentary. For us, Patton is engaged in a deceptively complicated interpretive effort. In *Nietzsche and Philosophy*, Deleuze says that 'interpretation reveals its complexity' when 'we realize that a new force can only appear and appropriate an object by putting on the mask of the forces already in possession of the object' (Deleuze, 1986, 7). We can read the montage-effect of Patton's work very much as an attempt to populate or appropriate the forces of a given object in order to make way for the appearance of a new force. The object in question, of course, is the discipline of political theory; the forces already in possession of the object are those, like liberal political philosophy, which dominate the discipline; and the new force, then, is the provocation of Deleuze and Guattari. In other words, Patton's writings performatively embody Deleuze's own Nietzschean suggestion that the work of interpretation is dramatic in form in that it entails the donning of appropriate masks. Deleuze and Guattari must be masked as normative political theorists of freedom in order to appear on stage but the effect of this is then to de-familiarize the theatrical context itself. That is to say, the mask is donned, but then it is subject to 'piercing' (Deleuze, 1986, 5).

Drama and political thought

Anticipating an argument that still needs to be developed in the chapters to follow, we nonetheless want to begin to establish the following claim at this point: *the method of dramatization in Deleuze and Guattari aims to determine the nature of political concepts and how we come to access, know and feel the resonance of political concepts.* So, in this sense, we see our contribution to the literature on the political theory of Deleuze and Guattari not so much as the attempt to create a montage-effect at the level of content but in rather more formal terms to explore what the montaging of concepts implies: that is, *an exploration of the conditions in and through which political concepts are brought to life.* For us, there is a drama that is played out beneath the formulation of political concepts, and the practice of political thought can be viewed anew when light is cast on this drama.

Of course, the idea that drama can serve as a medium for the expression of political thought is virtually co-extensive with the history of drama itself, from the early Greek plays to the recent theatrical re-enactments of politically charged public inquiries. Equally, the idea that political theory often contains dramatic elements and references within it is hardly contentious. For example, it has been said that Plato's *Republic* owes a 'debt to Aristophanic comedy' (Pappas, 2003, 14). There is also the growing recognition of the significance (Skinner, 2008) of Chapter sixteen of Hobbes's *Leviathan*, entitled 'Of Persons, Authors and things Personated', which contains important distinctions between persons, artificial persons and those artificial persons that 'have their words and actions owned by those whom they represent' that Hobbes calls 'actors' (Hobbes, 1968, 218). In a general sense, moreover, we are familiar with the political theorist as a kind of director, staging a situation for the reader that presents a dramatic version of the problem being addressed: consider again Taylor's dramatized scenario above – the forty-four year-old academic reflectively engaging in 'strong evaluation' ('Should I stay or should I go to Nepal?') – as a typically engaging example of how this can work. That said, it is clear that most political theory that employs dramatic elements does so without making any claim about the methodological importance of dramatization, viewing it instead as a simple heuristic or analogical device in the service of more traditional, interpretive and normative methods. Our intention in the present work is to make a stronger claim by insisting upon a methodological link between drama and political theory. This stronger claim undoubtedly begs a number of questions and attendant interpretive problems that we will have to deal with as the book unfolds.

Immediately, there is the problem of tracing the emergence and establishment of the method of dramatization in Deleuze and Guattari's individual and collective work. This is a task that we will undertake in chapter two. Those familiar with Deleuze and Guattari will immediately recognize that the method of dramatization originates in the writings of Deleuze rather than Guattari, finding its most explicit, comprehensive, perhaps even definitive, expression in texts such as *Nietzsche and Philosophy* and *Difference and Repetition*. However, we will show that while an explicit focus or discussion of the concept of dramatization comes and goes at various points, the *practicing* of the method (their actual dramatizing and bringing to life of concepts of various sorts) continues to operate across their collective body of work.

Also, there is the problem of framing our discussion of dramatization in methodological terms, and insisting on such a strong methodological link between drama and political thought. A host of further questions orbit around this broad problem, these include: why is it that, save the odd exception (Hardt, 1993; Boundas and Olkowski, 1994), scholars of Deleuze and Guattari have remained indifferent to the notion of dramatization as method?; is this because the very concept of 'method' is too overburdened with presuppositions that are incompatible with key elements of Deleuze and Guattari's philosophy?; is it even possible or productive, then, to endeavour to locate a method in Deleuze and Guattari?; and if we can indeed productively engage with Deleuze and Guattari on these questions, in what sense can we consistently and cogently say dramatization is a rigorous method?; what does the method allow us to discover, access and know about the political concepts it is thought to bring to life? This problem of method (and these attending questions) brings into sharp relief the necessity of providing a strong philosophical defence of the method of dramatization. This will be our task in chapter three when we seek to articulate the principal ontological commitments that sustain the method as such.

But before we tackle such specific problems and questions head-on in subsequent chapters, we think it would be useful to use the remainder of this chapter to keep our focus somewhat broader, providing a more general feel for some of the implications that follow from our task to establish and defend a Deleuze–Guattarian method of dramatization. This might seem a rather odd strategy of argumentation, in that we are putting the cart before the horse in suggesting the supposedly important implications that follow from an argument that is yet to be made. However, the pedagogical pay-off is that this strategy will hopefully allow us to anticipate the Deleuze–Guattarian method of dramatization in a way that makes it more resonant and immediate to scholars (political theorists or otherwise) who are not particularly familiar with Deleuze and Guattari, and who may then find that the very specific and technical aspects of our subsequent chapters leave them a little cold. This, of course, was the strategy of argumentation that we so admired in Patton. And we aspire, in our way, to his example.

So, what, then, could we say are the broad or more general implications that follow from developing and defending a Deleuze–Guattarian method of dramatization? We have already suggested that the tradition of political thought can be viewed anew as a particular kind of drama in the wake of Deleuze and Guattari. The implies that we engage in a specific kind of reading strategy when analyzing political theory, a method of reading that is particularly sensitive to the drama that is at play in the very formation of political concepts. There are two related aspects to this. First, and perhaps most obviously, there is a need to develop a critical sense that the medium, form or genre in which political concepts are formulated and expressed is immanently constitutive of their meaning and significance (Shapiro, 2002; Porter 2007). Second, though less obviously perhaps, the drama implied by the formulation of political ideas should fundamentally impact upon our sense as political theorists of what is involved in the process of conceptualization itself. The practical and critical nature of this process is, as we indicated earlier, based on a set of philosophical or ontological assumptions that require us to think of it as a necessarily aesthetic activity. Put all too simply: what we may think of as the aesthetic dimensions of political thought (say, the form, medium or genre of its expression) are not contingent or inessential, but necessary and constitutive. While fuller discussion of the philosophical-political implications that follow from this essentially aesthetic conception of political thought will be undertaken in subsequent chapters, we can nonetheless begin to give a sense of what this might mean by way of a particular example. The example we have mind is Habermas' well-known discussion of the distinction between 'communicative action' which is 'oriented to mutual understanding' and the 'instrumental use of language', understood as a feature of 'strategic action'.

Dramatic conditions

Those familiar with Habermas will know that this conceptual distinction, mapped out most extensively in his *Theory of Communicative Action*, is of the utmost significance to the Habermasian project, providing, as it does, the important foundation upon which his moral and political theory is built (for example, O'Neill, 1997). Of course, much ink has been spilled (and rightly so) by political theorists of differing hues in critically evaluating the detail of Habermas' theory of communicative action and the normative political theory that follows from it (among others, McCarthy, 1978; Baynes, 1992; Honneth and Joas, 1991). Our aim is much more modest – to use this familiar argument or conceptual distinction between 'communicative action' and 'strategic action' as the raw material that will allow us to experiment with the reading strategy appropriate to Deleuze and Guattari's method of dramatization. The aim of this experiment is to begin to show that the presuppositions conditioning concept formation have a significant and dramatic role to play in the concepts that emerge: if the empty space of the theatre is already lit, for example, then certain theatrical decisions are already ruled out. Let us turn, then, to Habermas' argument as he develops it in *The Theory of Communicative Action*.

As is well known, Habermas starts out from the assumption that communicative action oriented to mutual understanding is fundamental and primordial, that it is always-already part of the pragmatics of our language-use as such (Habermas, 1979, 1). Or as he explicitly puts it: 'the use of language with an orientation to reaching understanding is the original mode of language use, upon which indirect understanding... and the instrumental use of language in general, are parasitic' (Habermas, 1984, 288). In order to sustain this qualitative distinction between communicative action 'oriented to reaching understanding' and the strategic or 'instrumental use of language' Habermas draws on, and reconstructs, Austin's (1975) well-known differentiation of 'illocutionary' and 'perlocutionary' speech acts. 'Through illocutionary acts', says Habermas following Austin, 'the speaker performs an action in saying something' (Habermas, 1984, 289). The significance of illocutionary acts is their 'self-sufficiency'; that is, 'the speech act is to be understood in the sense that the communicative intent of the speaker and the illocutionary aim he is pursuing follow from the manifest meaning of what is said' (Habermas, 1984, 289). Perlocutionary speech acts function to bring about 'effects' on the addressee. 'The effects ensue whenever a speaker acts with an orientation to success and thereby instrumentalizes speech acts for purposes that are only contingently related to the meaning of what is said' (Habermas, 1984, 289). It is important to be clear that Habermas is not simply suggesting that speech acts can produce all manner of side effects that the language-user cannot envisage. This 'trivial', as Habermas sometimes calls it, characterization of perlocutionary speech acts needs to be supplemented by a more substantive acknowledgement of how they can operate with the 'design', 'intention' or 'purpose' of producing particular effects on an audience (Habermas, 1984, 289–90). This, of course, is why Habermas calls this form of language-use 'strategic' or 'teleological'; it is designed to bring about or realize certain intended ends or goals in social interaction.

So, how does this help Habermas justify his claim that communicative action 'with an orientation to reaching understanding is the original mode of language use' and that the 'instrumental use of language' is 'parasitic' on it? Habermas' claim, in the first instance, is a simple one: any attempt to engage in the strategy of creating perlocutionary effects on an intended audience always-already implies the pursuit of illocutionary aims. All strategic or instrumentalizing action, in other words, must be formulated with a prior attitude to necessary understanding. Habermas argues:

> If the hearer failed to understand what the speaker was saying, a strategically acting speaker would not be able to bring the hearer,

by means of communicative acts, to behave in the desired way. To this extent ... 'language with an orientation to consequences' is not an original use of language but the subsumption of speech acts that serve illocutionary aims under conditions of action oriented to success. (Habermas, 1984, 293)

This might seem a curious, rather counter-intuitive, argument, especially if we reflect on our everyday experiences as language-users. For surely there are instances in our everyday language-use when the illocutionary aims served in our speech acts are manifestly oriented to success above all else, rather than to any understanding. Think of the explicit imperatives that we issue to one another, the imperatives that are set down for us to follow ('Eat your food!', 'Close the window!, 'Pass the salt!', 'Please be quiet!'). Habermas does indeed realize that in issuing such imperatives the speech actor is simply making manifest a demand that is willed only in order to be obeyed; he recognizes that 'not all illocutionary acts are constitutive for communicative action' (Habermas, 1984, 305). And in light of this, he suggests that illocutionary speech acts constitute communicative action oriented to understanding only in as much as they raise 'criticizable validity claims', as he terms them. Imperatives do not raise such claims; they are demands pure and simple. That is to say, when we as speech actors find ourselves on the receiving end of imperatives, we 'cannot take a grounded position' in relation to the demands being made of us; we have no opportunity to 'adopt rationally motivated "yes" or "no" positions on the utterances of speakers' (Habermas, 1984, 306). For Habermas, it is this ability and freedom to say yes or no, to critique or even out-rightly reject the claims put forward by others in dialogical exchanges, that importantly defines communicative action as a contested, critical, reflexive and deliberative space, a space where, in principle at least, the force of better, or more rational, argument should carry the day. Such is the provocation of Habermas' pragmatics, a provocation he clarifies and dramatizes in the following way:

Whoever enters into discussion with the serious intention of becoming convinced of something through dialogue with others has to presume performatively that the participants allow their "yes" or "no" to be determined solely by the force of the better argument. However, with this they assume – normally in a counter-factual way – a speech situation that satisfies improbable conditions: openness to the public, inclusiveness, equal rights to participation, immunization against external or inherent compulsion, as well as the participant's orientation toward reaching understanding.... In these unavoidable presuppositions of argumentation, the intuition is expressed that true propositions are resistant to spatially, socially, and temporally unconstrained attempts to refute them. What we hold to be true has to be defendable on the basis of good reasons, not merely in...context but in all possible contexts, that is, at any time and against anybody. (Habermas, 2000, 46)

What we find Habermas defending in the above passage is his famous 'ideal speech situation', or, as he qualifies it here, the 'unavoidable presuppositions' (namely; 'openness', 'inclusiveness' 'equality' and so on) that are taken to inform and give shape to the deliberative and dialogical space that is communicative action. This shift in terminology is important from a Habermasian perspective as he is at pains to emphasize, time and again, that the 'ideal speech situation' is poorly or mischievously understood as an abstraction or idealization that is irrelevant to actual social life as we experience it. As is well known, critics of Habermas have long insisted that his notion of an ideal speech situation harbours within it a transcendental, perhaps even quasi-religious, yearning for something beyond the particular rough-and-tumble of dialogical exchange (interestingly, Habermas speaks of the 'linguistification of the sacred' in *Theory of Communicative Action*). This something might be referred to as 'the true', and we note from above that Habermas does indeed provocatively insist on the idea of the true being, as he says, 'defendable on the basis of good reasons, not merely in...[one] context but in all possible contexts, that is, at any time and against anybody'. Of course, the critical-sceptical response here is to say that this transcendental yearning for a truth beyond context, this desire for a 'mode of unconditionality' as Habermas calls it, is 'unhealthy, because the price of unconditionality is irrelevance to practice' (Rorty, 2000, 2). Habermas' response to this critique is of real interest, for us particularly, as it begins to bring into focus the drama at play in his defence of communicative action.

Most immediately, Habermas insists that both context and its transcendence are mutually presupposing tendencies immanent to communicative action. So, say, the notion of the 'truth' emerges from within the context of actual dialogical exchanges and experiences and yet points beyond this particular action context. That is to say, when we, as actors oriented to mutual understanding, raise validity claims concerning the truth of propositions, we are inevitably dependent on a communicative context to facilitate our utterances. And yet, in order for such action-oriented validity claims to be deemed true they need to be simultaneously justified in a manner that transcendentally points beyond the given context of justification. What makes Habermas' argument particularly provocative here is that he insists on this moment of transcendence or 'unconditionality' by suggesting it is a matter of 'practical necessity'. What could he possibly mean by this? Here is the argument:

> There is a *practical* necessity to relying on what is unconditionally held-to-be-true. This mode of unconditionally holding-to-be-true is reflected on the discursive level in the connotations of truth claims that point beyond the given context of justification and require the supposition of ideal justificatory conditions.... For this reason, the process of justification can be guided by a notion of truth that *transcends justification* although it is *always already operatively effective in the realm of action.* (Habermas, 2000, 49)

Therefore, to Rorty's sceptical remark that holding to truth or any 'mode of unconditionality' is 'unhealthy' and 'irrelevant to practice', Habermas responds with an insistence on its 'practical necessity' as such. But, how does Habermas make this claim work? Well, one of the ways to do this is simply to keep reinforcing or insisting on the notion that communicative action oriented to mutual understanding is, as he says above, 'always already operatively effective in the realm of action'. A good example of this resolute insistence can be found at one, rather dramatic, point in *Moral Consciousness and Communicative Action* when Habermas seems to say that communicative action always-already asserts its fundamental importance in practical social interaction precisely because it immanently plays through the formation of our subjectivity and the reproduction of our forms of social life. This (and our discussion of Habermas comes full circle at this point) is another way in which Habermas emphasizes the 'priority' of communicative action over the strategic or instrumentalizing use of language. He writes:

> Individuals acquire and sustain their identity by appropriating traditions, belonging to social groups, and taking part in socializing interaction. This is why, they, as individuals, have a choice between communicative and strategic action only in an abstract sense, i.e., in individual cases. They do not have the option of long-term absence from contexts of action oriented toward reaching an understanding.

This would mean regressing to the monadic isolation of strategic action, or schizophrenia and suicide. In the long run such absence is self-destructive. (Habermas, 1990, 199)

The aesthetics of political theory: or, reading the drama

As we have said, one of the important implications that follow from developing and defending a Deleuze–Guattarian method of dramatization is that it allows us to bring into clearer focus the aesthetic dimensions of political thought, seeing aesthetics as essential and necessary to its constitution as such. The case study of Habermas' defence of the priority of communicative action detailed above provides an example of how this can begin to work; or, more particularly, how we might develop a method or strategy for reading political theory as drama. Immediately, we are moved to focus on Habermas' use of language, the literary or linguistic form of his argument as such. If we are to read Habermas as a dramatist of political concepts, then the medium or form of his dramatization is undoubtedly language itself. Language plays a dramatic and significant role in the conceptual architecture built up by Habermas and is clearly the foundation on which his particular brand of normative political theory is constructed. We see evidence of this in the quote from *Moral Consciousness and Communicative Action* above; Habermas simply assumes that language is the key medium through which political subjectivity and the reproduction of social life are expressed. And the linguistic or rhetorical shape of his argument takes a curiously dramatic and problematic form here. Essentially, Habermas stages for his readers a seemingly stark choice, though it is not really a choice but an imperative. He says that as social actors we can choose to engage in 'strategic action only in an abstract sense' or in 'individual cases', and that we abstract ourselves from 'contexts of action oriented toward reaching understanding' only at the very high price of an 'monadic isolation' that, in the end, is 'self-destructive'. It is in this sense that the choice (communicative versus strategic action) is not really a choice at all, but an implied imperative or demand ('Engage in communicative action oriented to understanding or else you will become a schizo or suicidal!').

Now, if Habermas' explicit affirmation of the priority of communicative action rests, even in part, on the issuing of such an implied imperative, then we would seem to be in receipt of contradictory injunctions that are working against one another: he would seem to be rhetorically capturing his readers in what Gregory Bateson would call a 'double-bind' (Bateson, 2000, 61). That is to say, on the one hand, we are explicitly told by Habermas that all validity claims must remain, in principle, criticizable, whereby the communicative actor can rationally say 'yes' or 'no' to them in dialogical exchanges. While, on the other hand, it is made clear that we can never really be a position to consistently say 'no' (or indeed 'yes') to the proposition that communicative action oriented to mutual understanding is fundamental and immanent to our sense of self and the reproduction of our social life. This is a claim or assertion that is willed simply to be followed and accepted as such: a non-negotiable imperative or order that cannot be anything other than what Habermas would understand as a 'strategic' form of language-use.

Read through a Deleuze–Guattarian lens, Habermas' conceptual distinction between communicative action and strategic action does not, and cannot, hold, precisely because all language-use pragmatically functions through the issuing of such implicit imperatives, or what they would call 'order-words' or 'slogans'. We will discuss Deleuze and Guattari's concept of the 'slogan' or 'order-word' in chapter four, but we can already get some hints, through Habermas, about how such a notion might work. So when Habermas explicitly formulates the priority of communicative action in *Moral Consciousness and Communicative Action* this clearly implies that we simply recognize the order of things he identifies; the practical necessity and foundational role that he attributes to action oriented to mutual understanding. This then implies any number of further imperatives or 'order-words' (think, for now, of 'order-words' simply as imperatives; as a form of language-use that essentially aims to compel obedience), and these could include (among others): that we simply accept political subjectivity and the reproduction of social life are communicatively mediated in a fundamental way; that we simply go along with the proposition that our communicatively mediated social relations unavoidably follow a particular logic of argumentation (namely, one defined by an 'openness to the public, inclusiveness, equal rights to participation' and so on); that we see as imperative the need to enter into dialogue with the sincere and serious intention of becoming convinced only by the 'force of the better argument'.

The purpose of focusing on Habermas was not simply to add to the already well-established critical literature on the theory of communicative action. As we said earlier, our more modest aim was to use his familiar argument or conceptual distinction between 'communicative action' and 'strategic action' as the raw material to allow us to experiment with a reading strategy appropriate to our Deleuze–Guattarian method of dramatization. This we have done by paying some attention to the literary-aesthetic form of his key claims (the notion of a 'double-bind', operating both implicitly and explicitly as contradictory injunctions staged for the reader). This, of course, is an important aspect of the method of dramatization as a critical sensitivity to the medium, genre, or aesthetic form in which political concepts are expressed becomes crucial to grasping their meaning and significance. It is no accident, therefore, that one of the key problems and provocations posed by Habermas' argument in favour of communicative action (namely, the very possibility of maintaining its priority and insisting that the instrumental use of language or strategic action is parasitic on it) gets dramatized and brought to life by way of a linguistic and rhetorical form that restages it, but nonetheless in an inverted or curiously antagonistic form. That is to say, Habermas' argument itself becomes parasitic on the non-negotiable 'order-words' or imperatives that strategically and *dramatically* sustain its conceptualization from the first instance.

And this is hardly just a matter of Habermas employing a particular dramatic or rhetorical strategy (say, staging the stark choice between a life of communicative action as against the isolation and self-destructive abstraction of strategic action) to render more concrete the stakes of his argument. The link between the drama being played out and his formulated concepts is more significant than that, and the dramatic element of the conceptualization is understood only in a limited way for as long as we rest content with the idea that it operates as a heuristic or analogical device which makes communication and understanding (of the implications of the argument) easier. For the drama played out in Habermas' conceptualization of the priority of communicative action can also be made to orbit around, what we want to call, a more formal set of meta-political assumptions concerning how political concepts are conditioned as such. For example, we have seen how Habermas insists, against Rorty and other sceptics, on a notion of 'unconditionality' or 'truth', how 'the mode of unconditionally holding-to-be-true' is something we performatively take up when engaging in communicative action oriented to understanding. To repeat Habermas' key point: there is a 'practical necessity' to relying on something akin to a moment of unconditionality or truth as this is always-already operatively effective in the realm of social interaction as an 'unavoidable' presupposition of argumentation. Of course, Habermas can insist on such unavoidable presuppositions of argumentation by way of his claim as to the priority of communicative action, which we have seen dramatized in the manner above. This dramatization can be then seen to filter back through a variety of concepts, such as 'truth' and 'unconditionality', as their unavoidable condition. Put crudely; the concept of truth is staged and conditioned in and through its performance in a specific communicative context, a drama that then extends out by becoming the normative promise of a claim that is defendable in all possible contexts to a (virtually or potentially) universal audience.

At this point, therefore, we can see the drama played out in the Habermasian text beginning to take on the formal modality of the method of dramatization as we will develop it, implying, as it does, a consideration of how concepts are conditioned, brought to life and made to function. And we hope that the specific reading of Habermas undertaken here has given some sense of the potentially broader value and significance of developing and defending a Deleuze–Guattarian method of dramatization. As we have said, our (at this point speculative) wager is that a successful defence of dramatization as method can open the door to any number of new strategies of reading the canon of political thought, as well as contemporary political theory, as drama. For us, it is important to insist continually on the idea that there is a significant and constitutive aesthetic moment or dimension to political theory, and that the method of dramatization to be found in Deleuze and Guattari provides a useful (though, obviously by no means exclusive) way of thinking about this. Why is this important?

Well, for one thing, political concepts may then begin to take flight from their more familiar terrain: for instance, from the historical canon of political thought, or the dominant disciplinary modes and critical methodologies of contemporary political theory (such as the communicative, Habermasian-inflected, turns that animate and encircle so much of normative liberal political philosophy). This could result in opening us up to the realization that the formation and dramatization of political concepts extends well beyond such a terrain, and is indeed all around us, being densely woven into the fabric of everyday life and culture. In other words, the method of dramatization in Deleuze and Guattari could (and should) spur us on to develop a real acute and *critical* sensitivity to the ways in which political concepts emerge from a range of places, and how they come to us in a variety of aesthetic and cultural forms or genres. We will undoubtedly make some gestures in this direction as the book unfolds, particularly in the second half: for example, in chapter four, when we emphasize how a contemporary social-political formation like Belfast has been conceptualized and dramatized as a 'post-conflict' city by way of various cultural-media forms; or, in chapter five, when we show how a mainstream Hollywood film like *Boogie Nights* can be thought to dramatize and conceptualize the relation between cinematic production and flows of money. But before all that, of course, it is necessary that we finally direct ourselves to the more urgent task of establishing and defending the method of dramatization we have been anticipating in this chapter. This, then, will be our focus in the next two chapters.

2
Dramatization as Critical Method

In the previous chapter we argued that Deleuze and Guattari can be considered as political philosophers. There are three aspects to this worth re-emphasizing here. First, they engage in conceptual debates, around the notion of freedom for example, that are the stock-in-trade of political philosophers. Secondly, they offer a social theoretical understanding of politics that situates our grasp of political concepts (or, otherwise more generally put, 'the political') on a dramatic terrain that then allows us to begin to question the priority of a certain kind of communicatively grounded normative political theory (for instance, the typically Anglo-American variety that has been significantly shaped by a thinker like Habermas). On both counts, their work can be said to contain novel and compelling analyses, as shown by many of the commentators who pursue these avenues of research, their goal being the integration of Deleuze and Guattari into the canon of political theory. However, we have also implied, thirdly, that this integration will remain partial to the extent that it does not recognize the potential methodological impact of Deleuze and Guattari within political theory. Their work challenges the way we do political theory and the way that we think about the political; in these respects, it has the potential to make a contribution to the discipline every bit as significant as that of those proponents of the communicative turn who have dominated debates during the latter half of twentieth century political thought (MacKenzie, 2000). Indeed, we speculatively ended the previous chapter by suggesting that we could develop this challenge if we situated their account of dramatization as method more broadly within the domain of critical methodologies.

In light of this, two questions come into view. What does it mean to say that dramatization is a critical method? To what extent is dramatization the methodological guiding thread that runs through Deleuze and Guattari's contributions to philosophy and political theory? These questions will serve as the basis for the discussion in this chapter. That said, the full ramifications of treating dramatization as a critical method will only emerge as the ontological presuppositions of this method are teased out in chapter three. For now, it is enough to establish the terrain within which we wish to situate Deleuze and Guattari's contribution to political thought and to assess the complications and tensions that emerge when one prioritizes dramatization within their singly and collectively authored output.

From method to critical methods

In a Cartesian spirit, it is often remarked that sound method is that which distinguishes knowledge about politics from the opinions that make up the world of politics. While the journey of this idea through Western political thought is complex and contested, as witnessed by the subtle hermeneutical narratives of Gadamer and Taylor for example (Taylor, 1989; Gadamer, 1975), there is no doubt that it contributed to the rise of political science as the core concern of the discipline of politics from the late 1950s onwards (Marsh and Stoker, 1995). The aim of political science was to use the methods of the natural sciences to study political life. Broadly speaking and without covering over the nuances and internal tensions that exist within political science, two methods have come to dominate. First, there is the inductive empirical method that emphasizes rigorous observation of the political world and careful extrapolation of those observations leading to generalizable laws. This is the approach taken by many in the field of comparative politics. Secondly, there is the deductive rationalist approach that models political life on the basis of certain assumptions concerning how key or privileged agents interact in political life. This is an approach taken by game-theorists of various sorts who seek to analyze, for example, electoral behaviour patterns. Both these versions of political science take a naturalist epistemological stance: that we can know the political world by proper application of methods in the natural sciences. They simply disagree about what the 'science' in political science really means.

Alongside the emergence of political science in the field of politics the critique of this naturalistic attitude also emerged. Most notably, the interpretivists challenged the claims of naturalism in the social sciences (Marsh and Stoker, 1995). Chief amongst these critics of naturalism were Gadamer (1975), Ricoeur (1981), Taylor (1985a, 1985b, 1989) and MacIntyre (1981). The interpretivists typically drew upon hermeneutic philosophies that prioritized the intrinsic and in-eliminable interpretive dimension of every claim about the social and political world. Whereas political scientists view the world of politics as one that can, with due rigour, be treated as an object to be studied, the interpretivists argued that this failed to recognize that, in Taylor's famous phrase, human beings are 'self-interpreting animals' (Taylor, 1985a). In other words, the social and political world cannot be studied scientifically because the object of study, 'we humans', is already laden with values and meanings that are not of the same ontological status as matter, energy, and such like.

The legacy of the naturalist–interpretivist debates is manifold. Speaking broadly, they had two important consequences within political science. On the one hand, it led to deeper entrenchment within those of a scientific attitude: ever more refined and increasingly technical means were found to defend, as they would see it, the claims of rigorously generated knowledge about the political world. On the other hand, those of a scientific bent who nonetheless recognized the importance of the interpretivist challenge sought ways in which the values and meanings intrinsic to human behaviour could be measured and observed while remaining wedded to the general project of a science of politics. This response gave rise to much of what we call qualitative method in political science, methods that have developed variously sophisticated ways of garnering qualitative data through interviews, focus groups and small-*n* studies (Devine, 1995).

Within political theory there was a similar two-fold entrenchment. In their desire to define a role for political thought alongside but not subservient to that of the increasingly dominant political science, many of those influenced by the interpretivist criticisms turned either to the history of political thought, through the study of classic texts in their context, or to increasingly abstract and technical forms of moral philosophy. In other words, the value of political thought was to be found in other disciplines – history or philosophy – given that thinking about politics had become so scientific.

Of course, this was not the aim of the interpretivists themselves, nor was it the journey that they undertook in their work. Alive to the hermeneutic potential of excavating the sources of our moral views in order to evaluate the moral legitimacy (or not) of current norms, they retained a strongly critical edge. Notably, they all developed a critique of contemporary liberalism (mostly) from within that tradition itself (MacIntyre being the exception). This brought to light critical elements within liberal political thought that find their roots in Rousseau and Hegel rather than in the individualism of Hobbes and Locke. Such hermeneutic excavations of critical positions within liberalism linked their methodological concerns with their substantive political thought, and in making them they did much to contribute to the communicative turn in political philosophy.

A part of the linguistic turn that dominated twentieth century philosophy, the communicative turn in political philosophy is premised upon the idea that knowledge of the political world will only be revealed by engaging in a process of communication between free and equal interlocutors (MacKenzie, 2000). We have seen how this idea is at the forefront of Habermas' analysis in the previous chapter. From the perspective of method, the problem that Habermas identifies with the interpretivists, of a hermeneutic variety, is that they have insufficient grounds for the critical analysis of those processes of communication. In many respects, his theory of communicative action is his attempt at providing those grounds. It is a debate that has its roots in the critical tradition that spans Kant, Hegel and Marx (for instance, see Habermas, 1990).

Much has been said about these roots and this is not the place to rehearse the debates. For us, however, a key question that crystallizes out of these debates can be framed in the following terms: is it enough to interpret what people mean by excavating the sources of those meanings in the ideas that litter the past, or can these meanings be subjected to rational criticism on the basis of universal features of our communicative interaction? Or, to refine the question: if the ways in which we communicate with each other in advanced liberal capitalist societies are distorted, as Habermas claims, by money and power, then to what extent do these universal features contribute to the project of grounding the project of Enlightenment such that we can pursue more rational forms of social and political life? Methodologically speaking, then, can we access the internal dynamics of the political world through a non-naturalist yet rationalist interrogation of the norms of our interaction?

There is an echo in these questions of Marx's famous rebuke to Hegel (and his fellow young-Hegelians) in thesis eleven of his Theses on Feuerbach: 'philosophers have only interpreted the world in various ways, the point is to change it' (McLellan, 2000, 173). Indeed, in many respects, the tradition of critical theory of which Habermas remains the leading light, is indelibly marked by attempts to ground rationally defensible yet critical interventions that change contemporary liberal capitalist societies for the better. Yet, it is notable that Marx's thesis eleven does not contain the phrase, 'for the better'. This reminds us that there is a critical tradition that also finds sources in the modern philosophical tradition that holds normative implications in suspense. On this account, a critical method is one in which we come to know the world through changing it; whether or not this change will be 'for the better' is a question of a different order. There are comments within Marx that lend themselves to this methodological approach, not least the occasions when he resisted the temptation to discuss what post-capitalist society would be like. As early as their *German Ideology*, Marx and Engels refer to communism as the movement that will only come to know capitalism in the process of dismantling it (Marx and Engels, 1974). Here, the concept of change has a clear epistemological flavour: we will know the world by changing it.

Filtered through Althusser's structuralist Marxism, this methodological principle has become a bulwark of poststructuralism. It is in this sense that we situate Deleuze and Guattari's method of dramatization as a critical method: *it is the acquisition of knowledge about the political world through the activity of changing it*. As we will see, this is not based on taken for granted sources of meaning nor on questionable universal features of communication, but on the epistemological potential of changing the political world through a process of intensification Deleuze called dramatization. Just what this means will be initially explored in the next section as we trace the complex meanderings of dramatization through the work of Deleuze and Guattari and in the next chapter as we dig deeply into the ontological claims that underpin this view of it as a critical method.

Dramatization in Deleuze and Guattari

Addressing the question of dramatization as method in Deleuze and Guattari raises two preliminary interpretive problems. On the one hand, there is the problem of where to situate the concept of dramatization in the collective output of Deleuze and Guattari. On the other hand, there is the problem of privileging the idea of method in relation to their work. It is important to clear the ground in relation to these matters so that the discussion of dramatization as method can begin in earnest.

Firstly, there is no doubt that dramatization as method originates in the writings of Deleuze rather than Guattari. Indeed, one can trace this method through Deleuze's work without the need for separate discussion of Guattari's individually authored texts, and this is the approach we will adopt. That said, one must include within Deleuze's body of work the collaborations with Guattari (Deleuze and Guattari, 1977;

1986; 1987; 1994). To claim, therefore, that dramatization is the method that orients the work of Deleuze *and* Guattari is already a rather complicated statement. Moreover, it is important to recognize that dramatization appears to have been subject to an internal critique, notably the challenge to the theatrical model of the unconscious and, by implication, to the dramatalogical method itself, as found in *Anti-Oedipus*. Nonetheless, we maintain that this reflection on the theatrical model of the unconscious is best thought of as a clarification rather than a critique – and what gets clarified (through Guattari's influence) are the political implications of the method. This also helps to support the view, which we hold, that dramatization makes an implicit but fundamental appearance in their last work together in the discussion of 'conceptual personae' in *What is Philosophy?* (Deleuze and Guattari, 1994). While this claim is not without its complications, as we will discuss, we maintain that dramatization is a methodological thread that runs through the philosophical work of Deleuze and Guattari. We forsake, therefore, any of the more inventive nomenclature that might attempt to capture their differing attitudes to this method or their changing views on the subject. Important discussions of the theoretical and interpretive complexities raised by Deleuze and Guattari's authorial practices can be found in Genosko (2002) and Stivale (1998).

Second, dramatization as method has not, with a few exceptions (for example, Boundas and Olkowski, 1994; Hardt, 1993), been foregrounded in interpretations of Deleuze and Guattari's *oeuvre*. In part, this may be the result of the complicated authorial background just mentioned, but it may also be because there is concern about locating 'a method' in Deleuze and Guattari; at least for those interpreters who see all methodologies as overburdened with presuppositions incompatible with a philosophy of difference. It is our view, on the contrary, that the method of dramatization not only occupies a pivotal place in Deleuze and Guattari's philosophical system (even though it appears, at the level of content at least, to have a relatively short-lived existence within their work) but it is also a method that is entirely consistent with the difference-oriented philosophy they construct. Moreover, there is nothing about method, per se, that disqualifies us from privileging it in our presentation of their work below. While there is more that could be said on this issue, and we will address some of the complexities under the heading of the problem of modernism, it is nonetheless important to know that it serves as a presupposition of our discussion that there is *a method* employed by Deleuze and Guattari that can be applied within political theory. With these two clarifications in place, we can proceed to see how the method of dramatization emerged from within Deleuze's engagement with certain central philosophical figures and themes.

Deleuze's (1991) early work on Hume, particularly *Empiricism and Subjectivity*, is characterized by a desire to resist the rationalist view that concepts express essences and that one can only understand the relation between concepts when one has first understood their respective essences. As clarified by Hayden, Humean empiricism for Deleuze is 'a theory of relations' that 'displaces the emphasis on essential characteristics and stresses instead that relations come into existence by practical rather than essential or necessary means' (Hayden, 1995, 302). If we add to this, as Deleuze does, the claim that concepts are intrinsically relational, then we have the basis for an empiricist displacement of the rationalist approach to the determination of concepts. That is, if all concepts express relations (to the extent that they group elements together under the concept and they always exist in relation to other concepts) and there is no rational necessity for the relations they express, then the determination of concepts must itself be a practical activity (rather than a merely theoretical activity aimed at unearthing the essential characteristics of the related elements). Of course, this does not determine the kind of practical activity involved in the determination of concepts. Indeed, one could follow Deleuze in many divergent directions from this opening empiricist claim. In our view, however, and with a view to the methodological implications of this position, an important connection can be made to an under-theorized aspect of Deleuze's work on Bergson.

We find in Deleuze's treatment of Bergson that this practical engagement with concepts can take surprising forms. For example, he follows Bergson (2004) in drawing our attention to the ways in which humour and the comic can determine through dramatizing, or bringing to life, concepts such as the 'moral law'. In the following passage, for instance, Deleuze lays out the possibility of humour and irony as forms of repetition that function in this way. He writes:

There are two known ways to overturn moral law. One is by ascending towards the principles: challenging the law as secondary, derived, borrowed...; denouncing it as involving a second-hand principle which diverts an original force or usurps an original power. The other way, by contrast, is to overturn the law by descending towards the consequences, to which one submits with a too-perfect attention to detail. By adopting the law, a falsely submissive soul manages to evade it and to taste pleasures it was supposed to forbid.

We can see this in demonstration by absurdity and working to rule, but also in forms of masochistic behaviour which mock by submission. The first way of overturning the law is ironic, where irony appears as an art of principles, of ascent towards the principles and of overturning principles. The second is humour, which is an art of consequences and descents, of suspensions and falls.... Repetition belongs to humour and irony; it is by nature transgression or exception. (Deleuze, 1994, 5)

Where irony plays with the forces and powers that give shape to the moral law, forces and powers that can be used to ridicule and usurp the tendency to speak about it in rather lofty terms, humour implies descent to its consequences, an excessive literalism that brings to life the essential contingency and absurdity of this concept. Both approaches privilege the relations expressed by the concept of the moral law and express those relations by drawing them out through a particular practical engagement. So we could say, taking one of Deleuze's own practical examples above, that a humorous or excessively literalist 'working-to-rule' allows those doing the 'working' to connect and determine laws or rules in relation to their attending contingencies and absurdities (think, for instance, of the various roles as 'workers' or other subordinates perfected by the great Laurel and Hardy – more on them below). And this example is obviously pertinent to our discussion because it shows that practical philosophical engagement can take the form of an artistic engagement – in this case, the art of humour. We will revisit the importance of humour to Deleuze's (and Guattari's) method of dramatization in chapter four, and we shall see how they dramatize concepts, and make arguments, through a form of language-use or writing that is explicitly, and self-reflexively, humorous.

For the moment, though, we need to keep our focus on clarifying and generalizing what is at stake in this practical engagement with concepts (humorous or otherwise). This we can do if we consider how it was further developed in Deleuze's work on Kant (Deleuze, 1984). It is well known that his book on Kant was 'a book on an enemy' but it is also becoming increasingly clear that Deleuze was deeply indebted to his enemy; in particular, to the extent that Deleuze articulated his theory of ideas as a realization of Kant's critical project (Kerslake, 2002 and 2009; Smith, 2006; McMahon, 2009). Deleuze can be characterized as a post-Kantian, in these two important respects: that things in themselves are not self-determining and as such philosophy's task is not to find the concepts that *represent* the self-determining nature of things (in this sense he is at one with the Kantian critical turn against dogmatism); and that ideas are necessarily indeterminate but nonetheless serve a practical role vis-à-vis concept formation. Deleuze criticizes Kant's 'Copernican turn', however, because in situating ideas in the remote reaches of our faculty of rational representation Kant claims that they can not be the object of any possible experience. It is not that Deleuze argues that we can simply experience ideas in their indeterminacy (that would be to create a dogmatism of the idea), but rather that the indeterminacy of ideas is a constant *problem* for our experience of the world. In other words, Deleuze treats ideas as real problems: as outside of yet productive (rather than inside and regulative) of thought. As elegantly summarized by McMahon, treating ideas as problems in this sense means that 'they confront and compel thought in virtue of their positive indeterminacy, an indeterminacy that nevertheless provokes thought to its highest powers of determination' (McMahon, 2009, 96); hence Deleuze's formal agreement with Kant that ideas have a practical role in the formation of concepts. On this account, the practical determination of concepts discussed above in relation to Hume and Bergson is accorded its full critical potential as the on-going engagement with, what we may call, 'problematic ideas' that provoke thought. We will discuss more fully what Deleuze means by an idea in the next chapter, but for now we can maintain that the practical nature of determining concepts is also, for Deleuze, a thoroughly critical task, in the Kantian sense of surpassing dogmatism (MacKenzie, 2004; Kerslake, 2009).

Before leaving Deleuze's treatment of Kantian critique there is one further insight that he draws from his 'enemy' that marks a crucial step towards the method of dramatization; namely, his interpretation of Kant's account of the 'aesthetic idea' (Kant, 1952). According to Deleuze, Kant recognizes that aesthetic judgments are precisely those that provoke thought by virtue of their indeterminacy; that is, they presuppose 'the existence of a free indeterminate accord' of the faculties (Deleuze, 1984, 60). Without going into the full ramifications of this insight, it is clear that Deleuze incorporates it into his general reconstruction of thought in *Difference in Repetition*. In other words, there is a necessarily aesthetic dimension to the practical and critical elements of conceptual determination developed through his engagement with Hume, Bergson and Kant. In general, Deleuze argues that we should move from determining the conceptual parameters of ideas to exciting the ideal yet indeterminate forces at work within concepts through a creative understanding of the task intrinsic to philosophy, namely thinking. All the pieces are now in place for Deleuze's explicit turn to the method of dramatization.

Deleuze's explicit articulation of the method of dramatization is first found in *Nietzsche and Philosophy*. In the three paragraphs that make up the section 'Nietzsche's Method', the method of dramatization is presented as the only one 'adequate to Nietzsche's project and to the form of the questions that he puts: a differential, typological and genealogical method' (Deleuze, 1986, 79). Moreover, addressing the possibility that bringing philosophical questions and concepts to life by creating characters appropriate to them, as Nietzsche does, may tend towards 'anthropologism', Deleuze argues that the transformations undergone by Nietzsche's characters always express forces at work that are unknown to man: 'the method of dramatization surpasses man on every side' (Deleuze, 1986, 79). Nietzsche's characters, according to Deleuze, must not be read as 'more-or-less' human as this de-dramatizes the ideal forces at work by referring them back to a fixed, given, 'dead', idea of the human. The importance of this in Deleuze's reading of Nietzsche is confirmed in his contribution to a colloquium on Nietzsche in 1964. He concludes, Nietzsche 'not only wrote a philosophy of theatre, he also brought theatre into philosophy itself. And with it, he brought new means of expression to transform philosophy' (Deleuze, 2004, 127). At this stage in Deleuze's work the method of dramatization is firmly established as that approach to ideas whose indeterminate experience exceeds the subject, which sets them into motion through a process of intense characterization (what this intensification requires will be discussed as the book unfolds). Internalizing Nietzsche's philosophical dramas as the realization of Kantian critique, therefore, was a further decisive moment in the emergence of a recognizable method within his work.

The presentation of *Difference and Repetition* for his Doctorat d'Etat and the defence subsequently published under the title 'The Method of Dramatization' are the high-water mark of Deleuze's appeal to this method. It is at this time that Deleuze generalizes dramatization as the method proper to a philosophy of difference. Deleuze, particularly in *Difference and Repetition*, conceives of the philosopher as director and the philosophical text as a script with characters and roles that the reader-actor can re-enact. In the Kantian language that Deleuze often deploys, we can say that the experience of re-enactment forces us to determine the idea of the script differently from what we think it is by virtue of the necessarily indeterminate nature of the script that the performance expresses. Consider, in this regard and by way of example, Deleuze's discussion of the Kierkegaardian script, and in particular his character of the 'knight of faith':

> When Kierkegaard explains that the knight of faith so resembles a bourgeois in his Sunday best as to be capable of being mistaken for one, this philosophical instruction must be taken as the remark of a director showing how the knight of faith should be *played*. (Deleuze, 1994, 9)

According to Deleuze, Kierkegaard (and this, of course, could be equally said of Nietzsche, or even Marx) created characters to express philosophical concepts precisely because such characters could be enveloped in 'an emotional, physical and environmental background' that itself could not be the subject of representation (Williams, 2003, 45). And, for Deleuze, this is the reality of the concepts we use: they are always locked into a field of dynamic interactions; otherwise concepts would have no meaning or resonance for us at all and they would simply fall dead on the ground. There is, therefore, as he says, 'a drama beneath every logos' (Deleuze, 2004, 103) and it is the task of the method to uncover this drama. 'Given any concept, we can always discover its drama, and the concept would never be divided or specified in the world of representation without the dramatic dynamisms that thus determine it in a material system beneath all possible representation' (Deleuze, 2004, 93).

It is rare for Deleuze to refer explicitly to the method of dramatization after this period of intense institutional scrutiny. In the methodological reflections interspersed throughout his work after *Difference and Repetition*, we find two tendencies. On the one hand, there is a succession of different terms to describe the method he and Guattari employ, presented as a process of methodological refinement. On the other hand, these apparently different methods are discussed in ways that maintain a strong continuity with the methodological project Deleuze established during his apprenticeship in philosophy. Whatever the label used, and even when it is described as an internal critique of previous methods, there remains a fundamental commitment to the practical, critical and aesthetic determination of concepts. To this extent, the practice of dramatization as method serves as the undertow to the stream of terminological inventiveness on questions of method that flows through his work after *Difference and Repetition*, the collaborative work with Guattari, and his later work on art and cinema. It is to this period that we now turn before finishing this section with a discussion of link between dramatization and constructivism established in *What is Philosophy?*

With the appearance of *Logic of Sense* in the late 1960s Deleuze tends not to describe his method, to the extent that this term is used at all, as one of dramatization. In 'Gilles Deleuze Talks Philosophy', an interview given in 1969, Deleuze is clearly less wedded to dramatization and talks of the move towards 'serialism' that characterizes his discussion of sense. Reflecting on this text for the Italian edition that appeared in 1979, Deleuze describes changing his method between *Difference and Repetition* and *Logic of Sense* in order to avoid the traditional philosophical presuppositions with regard to heights and depths that he thinks still marked the former book (Deleuze, 2006, 65). He says that this led him to a new philosophy of the surface in *Logic of Sense*, and that as the 'concepts changed... so did the method, a type of serial method pertaining to surfaces' (Deleuze, 2006, 65). On the face of it, therefore, it would seem that there was a decisive methodological break between *Difference and Repetition* and *Logic of Sense*. However, it is worth looking more closely at this change of method before simply accepting that the period of dramatization was over.

The ten years between the French and Italian editions of *Logic of Sense* are marked by his collaboration with Guattari. In this collaborative work, Deleuze's early interest in the methodological potential of dramatizing philosophy appears to have undergone the internal critique that was then retrospectively imposed between these two editions of the text. It would be easy to surmise, therefore, that the critique of the method of dramatization came from or was cemented by his work with Guattari. Indeed, this critique is at its most explicit in *Anti-Oedipus*, their first work together. As we will show, though, it is by no means straightforward to assume that dramatization as method is rejected in this text. It is certainly true to say that in *Anti-Oedipus* the image of the unconscious as a theatre is roundly dismissed: psychoanalysis, say they, invests desire in 'an intimate familial theatre, the thèatre of private man' (Deleuze and Guattari, 1977, 305). Indeed, 'schizoanalysis must devote itself with all its strength to the necessary destructions. Destroying beliefs and representations, theatrical scenes' (Deleuze and Guattari, 1977, 314). And yet, even here there is more than a hint of the persistence of the dramatic method (as that which releases, in this instance, the pre-individual drama at work beneath the construction of Oedipal subjects). Deleuze and Guattari write:

> That is what the completion of the project is: not a promised land and a pre-existing land, but a world created in the process of its

tendency, its coming undone, its deterritorialization. The movement
of the theatre of cruelty: for it is the only theatre of production, there
where the flows cross the threshold of deterritorialization and produce a new land – not at all a hope, but a simple "finding", a "finished design", where the person who escapes causes other escapes,
and marks out a land while deterritorializing himself. An active point
of escape where the revolutionary machine, the artistic machine, the
scientific machine and (schizo) analytic machine become parts and
pieces of one another. (Deleuze and Guattari, 1977, 322)

The familial scenes discovered by psychoanalysis may well need destroying but the means to do this are to be found in a different kind of
theatre: the 'theatre of production' or 'theatre of cruelty' (Artaud, 1993).
And such is the case with *Logic of Sense*: after discussing his change of
method Deleuze nonetheless refers to his desire to employ serialism as
'a surface art'. The construction of concepts adequate to the paradoxes
of sense, therefore, is still an art for Deleuze (think again about the
importance of the art of humour for Deleuze, and particularly in the
context of *Logic of Sense*, as we shall see in chapter four); it is still rooted
in the journey towards dramatization that we have reconstructed from
his work on Hume to that of *Difference and Repetition*. If the theatre is
deemed to have too many connotations of heights and depths this is
a secondary issue to the actual use of the method of dramatization.
Indeed, in his 1979 account of the methodological relationship between
Logic of Sense and *Anti-Oedipus,* we can discern this constant reworking
of the key assumptions within an established frame of reference (importantly, this also anticipates the famous discussion of the rhizome in *A
Thousand Plateaus*):

> What happened to me since *Logic of Sense* now depends on my having
> met Felix Guattari, on my work with him, on what we do together. I
> believe Felix and I sought out new directions simply because we felt
> like doing so. *Anti-Oedipus* no longer has height, or depth or surface.
> In this book everything happens, is done, the intensities, the events,
> upon a sort of spherical body or scroll painting: the organless body.
> Together we would like to be the humpty-dumpty of philosophy, or
> its Laurel and Hardy. A philosophy-cinema. I believe also that this
> change of method brings with it a change of subject matter, or vice-
> versa, that a certain kind of politics takes the place of psychoanalysis.
> Such a method would also be a form of politics (a micropolitics) and
> of analysis (a schizoanalysis) and would propose the study of mul-
> tiplicities upon the different types of organless bodies. A rhizome

instead of a series, says Guattari. *Anti-Oedipus* is a good beginning, provided we can break away from it. (Deleuze, 2006, 65–6)

There a number of important points to draw out here. First, we can see that Deleuze understands the methodological importance of his collaborative venture with Guattari as one that took him away from dramatization and serialism to rhizomatics. This movement is described as one that gradually divests his method of traditional philosophical concerns with heights and depths and then with surfaces with a view to the establishment of a productive philosophical method of rhizomatic connectivity. It would appear, therefore, that Deleuze understood this movement, particularly as spurred by his work with Guattari, as one of internal methodological critique. Secondly, it is notable that this movement is described in terms that are resonant with the practically oriented critical approach to the determination of concepts that led Deleuze to dramatization in the first place. The internal critique, in other words, is described in terms that fit squarely within the methodological frame of dramatization. The move toward rhizomatics, therefore, is best understood as an attempt to meet the requirements of the method he established during his apprenticeship rather than an attempt to distance himself from it. The provocative notion that Deleuze and Guattari could become the Laurel and Hardy of philosophy, for example, makes perfect sense in the context of the dramatizing function of humour, which we mentioned above in relation to Deleuze's treatment of Bergson and which, to repeat, we will develop further in chapter four. This general openness to aesthetic forms in the determination of concepts is further reinforced by the reference to a 'philosophy-cinema', a notion that we will also pick up on later at some length in chapter five. For the moment, however, we can say that it is clear that the language of this move away from dramatization is thoroughly couched in terms of the analysis that led Deleuze to the method in the first instance. Thirdly, the real concern being expressed by Deleuze at this stage is with the model of the unconscious as a theatre (the critique we saw in *Anti-Oedipus*), not with the dramatization of concepts itself. The aim is to challenge the theatrical model as used within psychoanalysis rather than dramatic method as a means to the determination of concepts. Lastly, however, it should not go unremarked that there is a change of tone because, unlike the methodological reflections leading up to *Difference and Repetition*, method is now linked directly to a form of politics: 'micropolitics'. Indeed, the real impact of Guattari at the methodological level is not that he led Deleuze away from the traditional method of dramatization but that he brought Deleuze to the increasing realization (of course, already implied and indeed often explicit in Deleuze's pre-Guattari work) that the <u>practical critique of</u> <u>concepts through their dramatization is a political intervention, and</u> <u>one requiring an analytical and conceptual practice adequate to the</u> <u>political.</u> As Deleuze says in his preface to Guattari's posthumously published *Schizoanalytic Cartographies*: 'Felix introduced two main notions from the point of view of institutional analysis: group-subjects and (non-hierarchical) transversal relationships. As you can see, these notions are as political as they are psychiatric' (Deleuze, 2006, 382). Furthermore, the idea that Deleuze and Guattari began to foreground the political nature of the method of dramatization, for all that they introduced other labels, is borne out by their work together in the 1970s up to and including *A Thousand Plateaus*.

For us, one important aspect of Deleuze and Guattari's foregrounding of the political is their continuing stress that aesthetic ideas and forms should be located at the heart of political thought. That is to say, during the period of their collaboration, begun by *Anti-Oedipus*, they show a consistent desire to demonstrate the ways in which aesthetic forms can denaturalize the social and political differences that we take as natural. For instance, in *A Thousand Plateaus* they emphasize how painting can effect movements in thought that harness 'powers of becoming that belong to a different realm from that of Power and Domination' (Deleuze and Guattari, 1987, 105–6). In *Kafka*, to take but one other example, they insist that Kafka's fiction dramatizes 'a deterritorialization of the world that is itself political' (Deleuze and Guattari, 1986, 47). Time and again, Deleuze and Guattari locate various aesthetic forms at the heart of their philosophy of difference, and they attribute to these forms a particular power to dramatically effect movements in (political) thought. To this extent, we could say that Deleuze and Guattari engage in an 'aestheticization of political theory' (Porter, 2009).

This is a theme that Deleuze also put to work in his own writings on both the painter Francis Bacon and during his two books on cinema. In both cases, Deleuze turns to art forms with the hope of finding concepts that directly impact upon how we experience the world. Both painting and cinema, although replete with their own macropolitical agendas, have the potential to unleash micropolitical movements by virtue of creating concepts that express the intrinsically indeterminate nature of ideas. In *Cinema 2*, furthermore, he says that cinema introduces the viewer to 'a principle of indeterminability, of indiscernibility: we no longer know what is imaginary or real, physical or mental' (Deleuze,

1989, 7). In many respects, Deleuze understood the political impact of art as Proust had: 'Thanks to art, instead of seeing a single world, our own, we see it multiplied, and we have as many worlds at our disposal as there are artists, worlds more different from each other than those that spin through infinity'. (Deleuze, 2000, 187). Deleuze returns again and again to art, therefore, because these forms are necessarily political in that they multiply the 'worlds at our disposal' beyond the world that we assume is so natural.

While it clear that Deleuze found philosophical thought in artistic media such as painting and cinema, he also never relinquished the idea that philosophy itself could always be practiced in creative ways. The books on Foucault and Leibniz are exemplary in this regard (Deleuze, 1988b; 1993). They provide creative readings of these thinkers on the basis that they both created projects that could never be complete. It is no coincidence that the motif of the fold runs through them both. By way of this motif, Deleuze expresses the ways in which both Foucault and Leibniz never ceased experimenting with the movement of thought, always looking to find new ideas within and through the folding of thought. Just as an artist will revisit and redefine their practice again and again, so it is with the great thinkers, to the point where the practice of renewal, of folding in different directions, must be understood as the project itself. It is a project that he also discerned in Guattari's solo work: 'Felix reached an unusual level that contained the possibility of scientific functions, philosophical concepts, life experiences and artistic creation. This possibility is homogenous while the possibles are heterogeneous' (Deleuze, 2006, 382). The fold provides a way of combining the homogeneity of the project with the heterogeneity of its results. In his review of *The Fold*, Badiou recognized the importance of this image across Deleuze's *oeuvre*; it provides 'an antiextensional concept of the multiple', 'an antidialectic concept of the event' and 'an anti-Cartesian (or anti-Lacanian) concept of the subject' (Badiou, 1994, 51–59).

By the time of Deleuze and Guattari's last work, the idea that philosophy, art and politics must be folded together were so firmly entrenched in the minds of their readers that *What is Philosophy?* was both revelatory and shocking. It was revelatory to the extent that it grounded their philosophy in a constructivist method that seemed wholly in tune with their philosophical-political experimentation through the arts. It was shocking to the extent that it appeared to separate philosophy from art and that there was no apparent place for politics. It is to these issues that we now turn with a view to setting up some problems that will be addressed in later chapters (see also, Alliez, 2004; Mackenzie, 1997; 2004).

As is well known, in *What is Philosophy?* Deleuze and Guattari aim to establish that philosophy should not be thought of as a form of contemplation, reflection or communication, but rather as a form of creation. The prior three forms, they argue, are all versions of idealism because they seek to cover up the creative moment that inspires all philosophical activity with some form of necessity (whether in the 'object', the 'subject' or 'language'). Plato, for example, the arch-representative of contemplative objectivism, 'teaches the opposite of what he does: he creates concepts but needs to set them up as representing the uncreated that precedes them' (Deleuze and Guattari, 1994, 29). For Deleuze and Guattari, the task of a philosophical understanding of philosophy can only be met if it is first and foremost recognized that all philosophical concepts are created. A concept, though, is not simply that which 'surveys' the conceptual field (grouping certain forms of the state together, for instance); it also 'inaugurates' a plane of immanence (the idea that there is a world of states that can be thought about, for example). The importance of this two-fold implication of the concept is that it sharpens up the charge of idealism; idealist understandings of philosophy are those that confuse the concept and the plane, rendering both transcendental. So the task of avoiding the slide into idealism presents itself thus: we must keep separate that which the concept surveys and that which it inaugurates. But, how is this to be done? What must philosophical method look like if this confusion is to be overcome? In answering these questions Deleuze and Guattari invoke the 'conceptual persona' (Deleuze and Guattari, 1994, 61–83).

The conceptual persona is that which constitutes the relationship between the concept and the plane of immanence without subsuming the relationship under a pre-given identity of what it means to think. In this respect, the conceptual persona has the role of a methodological guiding principle. It serves as the 'point of view' that is established as the concept is created and the plane instituted. In a telling and little-discussed move within *What is Philosophy?* this point of view is generalized into the notion of territory, understood in the way that, say, French philosophy may be said to have a point of view, or, more broadly, the way that normative political philosophy brings a point of view to bear on the process of concept formation. These territories map out the methods that shape philosophical analysis, and when they become sedimented in thought they are the basis for the creation of philosophical knowledge. However, in becoming sedimented they equally serve to close off possible perspectives as the basis for the creation of further knowledge, and it is this that Deleuze and Guattari have in their sights. In contrast to those concerned with finding forms of knowledge that may be said to transcend perspective, their concern is this: how does perspective function to create knowledge?

In relation to our discussion this overview of their constructivist understanding of philosophy has important consequences. In general terms we can see how the practical, critical and artistic understanding of philosophical method developed by Deleuze as dramatization is allied to a non-idealist understanding of philosophy as a whole. In particular, the methodological implications are that constructivism requires the recognition of the perspective that one brings to concept formation, where this is understood as the foregrounding of the persona that animates the concept–plane relationship. In other words, the persona is the character that brings to life the relationship between thought and the non-thought that it implies. Nietzsche's characters are exemplary because they are 'explicit' (Deleuze and Guattari, 1994, 65), but all philosophical creators and all good philosophers are creators of concepts, have characters that dramatize the philosophical question of knowledge by bringing to life the perspective that relates concept to plane: the idiot, the doubter, the lover, the proletarian, the knight of faith, and so on. These characters personify the critic, even though they are never identical to the philosopher. In dramatizing the critic, the philosopher is able to establish a territory upon which the method becomes a critical method: a means of not merely interpreting a pre-given reality but changing that reality in the name of alternative forms of knowledge. As they say, 'Even the history of philosophy is completely without interest if it does not undertake to awaken a dormant concept and to play it again on a new stage' (Deleuze and Guattari, 1994, 83).

This explicit return to the method of dramatization, however, is not without its problems. There are two that are pertinent to our discussion: the relationship between philosophy and art and the seeming lack of a politics to their constructivism. First, in *What is Philosophy?* Deleuze and Guattari argue that philosophy is only one creative discipline and that art and science are equally creative though they do not create the same things. In relation to art, it is argued that artists create 'blocs of sensation' that institute 'a plane of composition' through the 'action of aesthetic figures' (Deleuze and Guattari, 1994, 197). There is, in other words, the same triadic movement of creation, but that which is created is different: philosophy and art are both creative disciplines but, they argue, we should not confuse them. This would seem to put a major obstacle in the way of our claim that dramatic method unites the practical and critical determination of concepts through artistic form. Secondly, this problem is compounded to the extent that there seems to be no systematic place for politics in their constructivism. To the extent that political philosophy does appear in this last work together, it is by way of a discussion of its utopian function; the conjunction of philosophy with the present milieu as the means to re-launch new struggles (Deleuze and Guattari, 1994, 100). The idea that the dramatization of concepts is necessarily political, in the sense that gave so much momentum to the work with Guattari, appears to have been displaced. Is it the case that the return of dramatization is also the return of a depoliticized method?

These two problems can be placed under the heading of the problem of modernism in Deleuze and Guattari. Is there a return to the modern form of differentiated critique that splits our knowledge of the world into different domains with different requirements? Is there a return to the idea of the depoliticized method that helped establish the priority of the naturalist position in the social sciences?

Throughout the rest of this book we will argue that this is not the case. The route to making this claim is not an easy one, however. On the one hand, it requires that we get to grips with the ontological claims supporting the dramatic method with a view to establishing this method as a critical method. On the other hand, it requires that we address head-on, so to speak, the ways in which this method can be put to work so that we can tackle the problems as they arise in context and with a view to resolving the issue by reworking the claims in the final chapter on dramatic events.

3
Dramatization: The Ontological Claims

In the previous chapter we developed the claim that dramatization can be understood as a critical method. We did so by first outlining what we mean by 'critical method' vis-à-vis the methods debates within political studies, and suggested that critical methods are those that see an intrinsic link between knowledge and change such that one comes to know the (political) world through the act of changing it. We then outlined the ways in which dramatization as method developed within the work of Deleuze's 'apprenticeship in philosophy' (Hardt, 1993). During this time it became a practical and critically oriented aesthetic model of how to determine concepts in ways that showed how those concepts are always open to revision rather than bearers of essences. We then continued to trace the influence of dramatization through Deleuze's collaboration with Guattari. This raised a number of complexities, not least surrounding the apparent critique of the dramatological model. We argued, however, that this critique was best thought of as a clarification of the method's political impact rather than a disavowal of dramatization itself. It was noted that this political agenda was played out in various ways in Deleuze's individual and Deleuze and Guattari's joint work through an engagement with the deterritorializing function of different aesthetic forms. We will return to (some of) these forms in more detail in Part Two as we consider how the method of dramatization can be put to work in relation to language, cinema and events. By the end of the previous chapter, through the discussion of *What is Philosophy?*, we argued that the constructivist model of philosophy and art it articulates can be read as both a return to the treatment of dramatization as method and as a formulation of it that raises certain problems in regard to our presentation. In particular, the apparent separation of philosophy and art as creative disciplines and the seeming lack of a systematic place for the political implications of the dramatic method raised concerns that Deleuze and Guattari, in their last work together, had surreptitiously returned to some of the modernist presuppositions regarding method that Deleuze's development of the practice of dramatization seemed to be challenging. In Part Two, we will use this as the motif around which to orient our discussions of how to put the method of dramatization to work in political theory.

From concepts to ideas...

Before that can be addressed, however, it is important to delve more deeply into dramatization to see what ontological presuppositions it carries with it. The aim of this chapter, therefore, is to systematize the claims of the method rather than chart its development and mutations within the *oeuvre* of Deleuze and Guattari. In doing so, we will have a better grasp of the issues driving the problems we have identified in the previous chapter and a better sense of how to resolve them. The questions that will guide our discussion in this chapter are these: in what sense is dramatization a method? In 'bringing concepts to life', what does this method 'discover'? In what sense does dramatization establish the relationship between knowledge and change so central to critical methodologies? What is the role of the aesthetic in this relationship?

The interpretation of Deleuze's early work on Hume, Bergson, Kant and Nietzsche established that dramatization is a practical and critical method for the determination of concepts as a form of aesthetic judgement. The method aims, therefore, to provide a creative appreciation of the conditions that give concepts their force or their quality rather than to establish their essence. What is meant by 'conditions' here? The conditions of any given concept are those that explain why it is pertinent, relevant and useful (or not) as a concept that provokes thought about the world and our place in it. This is not a feature of conceptual method that is at all foreign to traditional methodologies. Indeed, all methods (in social and political studies, certainly) require that the investigator establish the pertinence of the investigation before embarking upon it. However, this is usually treated as both a preliminary to the study and as something that is separate from the content of the study. For example, a study into the relationship between class and voting behaviour will have to establish that is a topic worthy of study, but then the arguments given to establish this will be put to one side so that the objective study of the relationship can be undertaken. From the perspective of dramatization and other critically oriented methods, this is a fallacious distinction. What is particular to dramatization is that it is the force and quality of concepts that the method seeks to determine.

But what are the ontological implications of trying to determine the force and quality of concepts? As Deleuze puts it, echoing Kant in the particular way we discussed in chapter two, the task of determining concepts is important because this is the means by which we can access ideas. An idea, for Deleuze, is 'in itself a system of differential relations and the result of a distribution of remarkable or singular points (ideal events)' (Deleuze, 2004, 94). In this chapter we will chart the argument behind this two-fold characterization of the idea: how do we understand the idea as first 'a system of differential relations' and second as 'the result' of ideal events? We will argue that accessing the differential relations that constitute the idea requires that this access take the form of an event such that *to know the idea one must constitute it differently*. As such, the dramatization of concepts is a method that enables access to the 'dynamic spatio-temporal determinations' (the differential relations) that constitute the terrain of the idea and, furthermore, this method requires the creation of difference within the idea itself in order to capture the dynamics within that terrain (the results of ideal events). As Deleuze puts it: 'We distinguish Ideas, concepts and dramas: the role of dramas is to specify concepts by incarnating the differential relations and singularities of an Idea' (Deleuze, 1994, 218).

We are well aware, though, that such Deleuzean terminology is of little help if it is not connected to our everyday experiences. When we talk in more everyday terms about drama we typically have in mind a work intended for performance: 'a state, situation, or group of events involving forces in opposition to each other', as glossed by the standard dictionary definition. In this sense, to qualify something as dramatic is to claim that it has a vivid, striking, heightened, illuminating or powerful affect. The dramatic sunset, for example, is that which stops us in our tracks, captures our imagination and illuminates our experience to the extent that we are almost forced to look at it. The verb form, to dramatize, has a related but typically more specific meaning. It is to discover the 'forces' within the novel, poem, text, painting etc. by making them vivid, by heightening them. Dramatization, therefore, even in common parlance is the process by which a text or situation is brought to life such that it effects a change in the emotional state of those involved (say, performers and spectators). The emotional impact of dramatization will come to be discussed below under the philosophical concept of intensity. Furthermore, in dramatizing a script, for example, we witness the creation of dramatis personae; this is the process whereby the characters in the text are 'brought to life' – given personae – not simply by the individual artist but through a complex combination of actorly, directorial, performative, contextual and other forces. As Deleuze argues in *Difference and Repetition*, this process of bringing to life or *performing the text* reveals more about the character (whether Kierkegaard's 'knight of faith', Nietzsche's 'superman', or Marx's 'proletarian', to take three examples he mentions in this context) than could be revealed simply by reading the text-script. In other words, there is, as is well known within theatre studies, a form of discovery in the playing of the part or the staging of the text; a discovery of the dynamic trajectories in which a character is implicated, for example, in the *particular* way that the character is performed and the play-script staged. Deleuze's claim, therefore, is that philosophical texts should not be read with a view to interpreting what they mean, but performed with the aim of bringing to life the forces that animate the text. In this sense we agree with Jones and Roffe when they say that Deleuze operates a consistent method of reading texts in the appropriation of those philosophers that constitute his 'philosophical lineage', but we disagree that this method is 'primarily a method of reading' (Jones and Roffe, 2009, 4) as this confuses the act of reading the text with the dramatic restaging of the text that is so central to his attempt to move beyond interpretation. As we will see, this clarification is necessary to the extent that we must always think through the ways in which dramatization links to a thought of the outside, a thought outside of philosophy itself that must be the constant source of its dramatic discoveries. But before we get ahead of ourselves, however, we must ask: what is being discovered in these moments of dramatization?

Deleuze argues that it is the *intensity of the character* (the concept, the text, etc.) that is discovered. Intensity is a key concept in Deleuze's philosophical lexicon and by no means one whose meaning is beyond dispute: witness the thorough commentaries and critiques it has spawned within the secondary literature on Deleuze (Boundas, 2009). For our part, and given the social and political theory context we are working within, we will typically think of intensity in very human terms, notably as the emotional domain that traverses human interaction and identity. Williams (2008; 2003) has made an art of explaining Deleuze's concept of intensity in this way. We can see what is at stake if we develop the idea in relation to our everyday understanding of drama.

Macbeth's monologues, for example, can be read on the page, and profitably so, if one is intent on understanding the rhythms of Shakespeare's language, the careful use of syntax and such like. But they demand an audience, an actor, a performance space, lighting (indeed, the whole panoply of elements at work in any dramatic production) if the intensity they contain is to be realized. We can say that Macbeth's monologues were written, but they were written to carry an emotional punch; that is, to be felt by the actor in their performance and by the audience in attendance. Indeed, anyone who has read Macbeth and then watched a well dramatized version of it will attest to the fact that previously obscure passages in the text can even become the most luminous aspects of the play when they are well performed. Generally speaking, any particular expression of the intensity of Macbeth's monologues will always depend upon the relations within which they are made manifest (there must always be an audience, for example, for the monologue). In this sense, dramatization as method is a method of intensification and it is the relationships between things – typically the emotional relationships between everyone involved – that are being brought to our attention either as performers or as spectators.

As it is with the characters of a play-script, so it is with the concepts of a philosophical text. In order to determine their force one must bring out their intensity by setting them within a series of conceptual, textual and performative relations rather than by seeking to determine their essence first and then seeing how they relate to other concepts. Deleuze understood from Hume that it is a fallacy of rationalism to think that the essence of concepts can be determined in advance of their manifestation within a particular domain of conceptual relations. For example, we should not assume that we know the essence of Macbeth's monologues in advance of their staging. It is more productive to work through the possible meanings they may contain in the process of bringing them to life as a series of relationships – that is, as a drama. As it stands, though, this rests upon the notion that the intensity we experience is always relational. Deleuze's ontological claim is more complicated and profound, however. For Deleuze, all the relations that we experience are *the result* of processes of intensification. In other words, it is not simply that things exist in a series of intense relationships; it is intensification that brings things into existing relationships. It is to this fundamental aspect of his philosophical system that we must now turn.

What is intensification? In the context of our discussion of method, intensification is the process constitutive of the extensive diversity implied by conceptualizations. While concepts group together elements that appear the same from the perspective of some criterion of identity, the point of creating the concept is to express the intensity of the elements that it groups together by bringing them into relations with each other. Clearly, this requires some explication and clarification. Returning to the play-script for a moment, we can say that the characters are conceptualized by being grouped together in a narrative structure, for example, but it is only through performance that one is able to distil the intensity of the relationships between them that their diverse roles in the narrative express. Drawing once more from the world of drama that we know, this is why performance groups tend to put so much emphasis upon the processes involved in bringing a play to the stage. It is no coincidence that many of the great innovations in dramatic practice are at the level of how performers come to embody the roles they have to play: the idea of method-acting springs immediately to mind, for example.

Putting on the play, in other words, is a process in which the process itself may significantly change the nature of the play that is produced. But does this make sense outside of the world of theatrical productions? We will pursue this in relation to politics towards the end of this chapter, but for now – with a view to showing the scope of this idea in Deleuze (and pointing to its genesis in his work) – we shall make a brief foray into the metaphysics of the natural world. One of Deleuze's favourite examples of intensification is the physical process of crystallization. It is an example that he drew from the work of Gilbert Simondon, a philosopher of science who is becoming increasingly recognized as one of Deleuze's most important sources (Toscano, 2009; Bergen, 2009). What happens as a crystalline solution precipitates individual crystals? One might argue that the individual crystals are already lying in wait within the solution ready, so to speak, to become the actual individuals they already are. However, as is clear from the science of crystallization, there is no way of saying in advance what particular crystals will form out of the solution, even the same solution. Given this, Simondon argued that we should treat the solution as a pre-individual field that acts as the 'ground' from which individual crystals are formed while not containing those individuals itself. The 'ground', in other words, is radically different from that which it supports – the individual crystals in this instance. But how does Simondon account for the emergence of individual crystals out of this pre-individual ground? He argues that we need to think of the process of individuation as one in which the pre-individual form of the solution informs the relationship between emergent crystals in an unpredictable way to create structured relationships between actual crystals. In amongst this difficult set of ideas is a profound claim that Deleuze sites at the heart of the ontological presuppositions that drive dramatization. When he asks himself, in chapter five of *Difference and Repetition*, how intensity can fulfil the role of constituting extensive relations, he turns to a gloss of Simondon's analysis: 'Gilbert Simondon has shown recently that individuation presupposes a metastable state – in other words, the existence of a "disparateness" such that there are at least two orders of magnitude or two scales of heterogeneous reality between which potentials are distributed.... Individuation is the act by which intensity determines differential relations to become actualized, along the lines of differentiation and within the qualities and extensities it creates' (Deleuze, 1994, 246). With a view to swimming back to the shore from the sea of these metaphysical claims we can say that the key point is that for Deleuze, following Simondon, when we think of individuals (people, performances and so on, as well as crystals) we must always remember that *process has primacy over product*.

It is a conclusion that is at the heart of, not least because it has informed, a wide array of contemporary art practice. Linking it back to our example of putting on a play we can see its importance. For our purposes, the solution can be read as the intense relationships that the script expresses and the individual crystals as the actual relationships between the characters that emerge in the process of crystallization. What is important, however, is not the latent relationships within the script (even though there are clearly a range of potential relationships) but how the actual relationships of any given performance emerge as the result of the process that they undergo. On this level, crystallization is dramatization, and vice-versa. The process of dramatizing the script establishes a series of relationships between *these* performers of *this* play in *this particular* context out of a script that could equally establish a different set of relationships if the process of dramatization was differently enacted.

How does this help us understand the relationship between concepts and ideas established in the method of dramatization? According to Deleuze, while concepts group together actual things by placing them in relation to each other, the process of conceptualizations, of forming concepts, is already a process of intensification such that all the relations that concepts express are already relations of intensity (Deleuze, 1994, 251). Furthermore, the relations that concepts express are contained within the idea from which they are drawn, just as the solution contains a variety of potential crystals and the script a variety of potential performances. The dramatization of concepts, therefore, requires setting them into relationships with each other in ways that express the intensity of the relationships they already express; it is a way of determining the idea that the concept expresses. As Deleuze puts it, 'intensity is the determinant in the process of actualization. It is intensity which dramatizes' (Deleuze, 1994, 245).

Nonetheless, we must be careful with this account of the ontological claims underpinning the method of dramatization, because it may give the impression that dramatization simply discovers the ideas that determine concepts in the rather traditional sense that layers of conceptualizations are excavated in order to unearth the pristine essence of the idea itself. Much of the recent work on Deleuze has sought to rectify this impression (Widder, 2001; Bergen, 2009), in part as a response to the critical literature that has promulgated it (Badiou, 2000; Žižek, 2004; Hallward, 2006). As stated at the beginning of this chapter, however, the method of dramatization has a second, 'evental' dimension that must also be appreciated. And we need to specify why this second aspect is required and what it brings to light in terms of the ontological claims that sustain dramatization as method. This demands a further foray into Deleuze's metaphysics of difference.

...and back again

We can begin by giving further consideration to the performance of Macbeth's monologues. Consider the teacher who understands that these monologues need to be performed to be understood, that it is not enough to simply read the text in search of its essence. She may choose the dramatic version that illuminated her own understanding so clearly as a student of Shakespeare, only to find that this same performance does little with the class she is now trying to enthuse. Something has happened here, and this happening needs to be understood if dramatization is to be given its full ontological status. First of all, it is important to recognize that this is not necessarily a failure on the part of the students; it is not that they simply don't 'get it' when they should. As is well understood in theatrical productions, the emotional intensity of Macbeth's monologues can only be determined through dramatizations that connect to the forces at work within the broader structures of performance and reception. While Olivier's renditions may have made sense to the teacher, for example, they may now appear archaic and alien to the students she is trying to provoke. The complicated forces at work within *and beyond* the play-script itself have changed such that Olivier's dramatization no longer appears relevant to the students. The dramatization of the text cannot ignore these broader structures of reception if the force of the characterization is to be brought back to life. Therefore, it is not simply a matter of performing the text well to unearth the idea that it contains; in order for it to be well performed it must be performed again, in a way that connects with the emotional background of the students. Given this, the ontological assumptions it imposes upon the method of dramatization are considerable. Indeed, if we accept that to dramatize is to express the intensive relations constitutive of concepts, and if we accept that this is achieved by putting concepts into relationships of intensity with each other, and if we accept that this requires different dramatizations dependent upon the structures of reception, then it makes sense to inquire more deeply into the nature of these intensive relations to see exactly what is at stake in this claim.

In our view, there are four key ontological claims that must be explicated if the method of dramatization is to be sustained. First, Deleuze argues that all relations of quantity and quality are conditioned by intensity: 'in short, there would no more be qualitative differences or differences in kind than there would be quantitative differences or differences of degree, if intensity were not capable of constituting the former in qualities and the later in extensity, even at the risk of appearing to extinguish itself in both', (Deleuze, 1994, 239: see Hughes, 2009, for an interesting discussion of how intensity cancels itself out). Second, he argues that intensive relations are relations of 'pure difference' – self-differing variations within things, so to speak, rather than the differences between things whose essence we think we already know. Deleuze argues throughout his work that intensive relations are not subsumable within models of difference that presume the pre-given identity of the related things. He argues that identity oriented definitions of difference (ones that view difference as opposition or contradiction, for example) always compare things against a pre-established view of 'the same' and thereby nullify difference. A non-identity oriented model of difference is one that can account for difference without the 'return of the same'. Summarizing rather dramatically, he concludes that in order to grasp the reality of pure difference we must view it as an intensive difference: a difference of intensity rather than a difference of extension (Deleuze, 1994; Deleuze, 1990). Third, he argues that intensive difference is always subject to a principle of indetermination. As noted in the previous chapter in the discussion of Deleuze's relation to Kant, indeterminacy is not something to be avoided in the Deleuzean metaphysical system. On the contrary, there is a necessity to recognize it as a condition of that which differs from itself, of 'pure difference'.

Deleuze uses the example of lightning to explain these three features of his explication of this different kind of difference: '... instead of something distinguished from something else, imagine something which distinguishes itself – and yet that from which it distinguishes itself does not distinguish itself from it. Lightning, for example, distinguishes itself from the black sky but must also trail it behind, as though it were distinguishing itself from that which does not distinguish itself from it', (Deleuze, 1994, 28). We experience the lightning flash as a moment of intensity before its illuminating quality and before we can quantify its luminescence. This intensity is not in opposition to the darkness from which it emerges (to say so would presume that darkness itself has no intensity); nor is it determinable vis-à-vis the intense nature of the darkness, because that has its own intensity (it does not make sense to say that the flash of lightning is the same as one hundred, or one thousand etc., moments of darkness). He concludes that: 'Difference is this state in which determination takes the form of unilateral distinction. We must therefore say that difference is made, or makes itself, as in the expression "make the difference"' (Deleuze, 1994, 28).

This idea of unilateral distinction is a Deleuzean formulation – one of many it must be said – that operates in the same way as Simondon's account of how process forms product. The flash of lightning, we may say, brings both the intensity of light and dark to our senses as part of the same process. Equally, the dramatization of the play brings us to our senses with regard to the script and the performance; we can see the play and read it again *differently*. From the perspective of the dramatization of concepts, we come to know the idea through the process of conceptualizations but in doing so we come to know the idea that the concept expresses differently. At every step of his metaphysical journey, Deleuze reminds us of the two-sided nature of this process. We are drawn to think about individuals (crystals, performances, concepts) through a process that expresses their link to the pre-individual domain (solution, script, idea) from which they emerge. But we can only think about this pre-individual domain by conceptualizing: we must access the process by performing it again, differently.

This brings us to the last important clarification of Deleuze's philosophy of difference (at least for our purposes of grasping dramatization as method). According to Deleuze, relations of pure difference are indeterminate (they have a role in determining individuals but cannot in themselves be determined) and, as such, they are an ideal but nonetheless real component of actual – determinable – things. Of course, 'ideal' here refers to Deleuze's materialist understanding of the idea (the solution and the script are ideal in this sense), and therefore it is imperative that it is not taken to imply any sense of perfection. Equally, Deleuzean ideas are not the 'property' of a unified subject, be it an individual person or a trans-historical spirit. As we have just seen, they are the pre-individual domain from which concepts are 'precipitated'. Rather, an idea, for Deleuze, is a distribution of differential relations, indeterminate in themselves but nonetheless productive of efforts to determine them (as we saw in the previous chapter with regard to his account of aesthetic experience derived from Kant). An idea, therefore, and as Deleuze is fond of saying, is not a set of concepts we employ to resolve a problem in our representation of the world; rather, an idea is a *real problem* that makes us think conceptually: it is 'an "objective" problematic field, determined by the distance between two heterogeneous orders' and 'the act of individuation consists not in suppressing the problem, but in integrating the elements of the disparateness into a state of coupling which ensures its internal resonance' (Deleuze, 1994, 246). It is real, or 'objective', as Deleuze tentatively puts it, in that it resides outside of us, as a provocation to thought. The idea is a problem to the extent that it is constituted as a system of differential relations that cannot (in principle) be determined once and for all. Ideas, we can say, are problems without any single solution, just as a solution in the physical sense is an idea without any single realization as a crystal formation. Borrowing the term from Bergson, Deleuze (Deleuze, 1988a) refers to the indeterminate yet real nature of ideas as *virtually* implicated in every *actual* attempt to determine them through conceptualizations. As such, Deleuze's ontological commitments lead him to argue that every determination of the real is conditioned by a virtual idea of that reality, just as every invocation of the virtual idea is conditioned by our attempts to understand it conceptually. Just as the performance of Macbeth's monologues is conditioned by Shakespeare's text, our understanding of the text is equally conditioned by every performance. As such, the important point to draw from this foray into Deleuze's metaphysics is that the relationship between the concept and the idea that it expresses is necessarily problematic – on the grounds that they are in a state of mutual conditioning that exhausts neither the concept nor the idea. The fundamental importance of this two-fold conditioning is eloquently generalized by Bergen (to the extent that 'nature' and 'ontology' here generalize the claims we have developed in the language of solution and crystal, script and performance, concept and idea):

> Ontology is not a mere illusion that plays with thought any more than thought would play with ontology. Nature is not what thought

takes from behind but rather what composes the wave of Being that it then rejoins. One thing among others attests, I think, the perdurance of the ontological question across Deleuze's work: the definition of the plane of consistency as that which ought to be thought and yet cannot be thought (*What is Philosophy?*) brings back the definition of the idea in *Difference and Repetition*: the rise of an ontological problem and of an unthought, which is both the thing most intimate to thought and also its absolute outside. (Bergen, 2009, 21)

This eloquently joins together the interpretation we gave in the previous chapter regarding the development of the method of dramatization and the claims we have articulated in this chapter with regard to the ontological position that serves as its ground. Notably, Bergen establishes the connection between dramatization and constructivism: we can now see that the relationship between the concept and the plane of immanence is crucial to this two-sided ontology of Deleuze, where the plane of immanence is simply another term that he uses to talk of the ideas that concepts presuppose. Crucially, from the point of view of method, the relationship between these sides is kept open by its problematic nature. This problematic nature is presented in Deleuze as the movement between these two domains, a movement that defines the conceptual persona of *What is Philosophy?*: namely, a movement on the open territories of perspective. Conceptualization always expresses an idea but it does so by taking a perspective on that idea: we always bring a persona to bear within the methods we use, and if we do not recognize this then we will tend toward idealism – the collapse of concept and idea.

This becomes clearer if we ask the following question: why does the method of dramatization express this intrinsically problematic nature of the idea while other methods do not reach the ideal problem they seek? Characteristically, Deleuze's answer to this question can be found in the connection he establishes between the method of dramatization and certain forms of question. In the defence of his Doctorat d'Etat, he puts it like this:

The Idea responds only to the call of certain questions.... The question what is this? prematurely judges the Idea as simplicity of the essence; from then on, it is inevitable that the simple essence includes the inessential, and includes it in essence and thus contradicts itself... [the Idea] can be determined only with the questions who? How? How much? Where and when? in which case? – forms that sketch the genuine spatio-temporal coordinates of the Idea. (Deleuze, 2004, 95–96; see also Deleuze, 1994, 246)

Now we can answer the question of how we dramatize a concept; we ask questions such as 'how much of it is there?', 'how much do we want it?', 'do we want it here, this much in this context but that much in another context?', 'should we use this concept now, but not then or in the future?' etc. The point is that this takes us to the frontiers of the concept, its moments of intense crystallization such that we are able to access the differential relations that make up the idea that it expresses – though only through this particular determination of the concept. Just as theatre directors and producers must ask whether or not it is worth restaging Macbeth now and here, so it is that methodologists must approach the concept they wish to analyze by recognizing that these questions are intrinsic to establishing a process that will define, in the end, the product or outcome of the study.

But isn't there still something obscure in all this? For how do we get to the moment of intensification within the concept through which we can 'discover' the differential relations? Williams captures what is at stake:

> An actual thing must change – become something different – in order to express something. Whereas, the expressed virtual thing does not change – only its relation to other virtual things, other intensities and Ideas change. This explains the conceptual innovations of *Difference and Repetition*. Deleuze has to introduce the concepts of multiplicities of pure differences and of envelopments of intensities to escape ways of thinking of change in terms of causal changes in parts that effect a whole. (Williams, 2003, 200)

Given the two-fold ontology of the virtual (yet real) intensities enveloped in all actual, extensive things, if we simply conceptualize things as they appear to us we will always miss that part of reality that conditions our experience of the thing itself: its intensity. Yet, in order to access this other (virtual) part of the thing itself we must change that which is actually present. In so doing, we will be able to reveal the forces at work within things, but we will also have impacted upon those forces, at the level of the ideal events that constitute them, and thereby we will have changed the idea itself that the concept expresses. To know the idea behind the concept, therefore, is to change the relations within and between concepts so as to express the system of the pure differential relations constitutive of the non-representational idea that conditions our determination of the concept. To put it as a slogan: *make an event of thought!*

We will return to this notion of the event in the last chapter and in doing so see that it plays a fundamental role in our attempt to secure the methodological link between *What is Philosophy?* and *Difference and Repetition* as a necessarily aesthetic link in a way that complements Bergen's account but nonetheless takes it in new directions. At present, it is enough to note that an event for Deleuze is not a mere occurrence; it is not just anything that happens (as it is within analytical philosophy). Rather, the event in Deleuze is a significant occurrence where significance is indicative of a change in the intensive relations of the ideas that constitute things. It is this idea of significance that has been lurking behind phrases such as 'the well dramatized play'. A play can be dramatized in a variety of ways that merely replay what is already known about the text. In this sense, and as theatre critics often point out, there is no point to the dramatization: it is of no significance. If the performance changes what we know about the text, by bringing out potential interpretations that have lain dormant within it, then we can say that it is a significant restaging of the text, one that has significance. Moreover, at least part of this significance is that it will change all future performances of the text, because in some way they must take account of this significant rethinking of what the text means, if only to disavow or distance any further production from it. Such performances are theatrical events because they are events in the general sense. To dramatize concepts in order to access the ideas they express, therefore, is to 'make a difference' by making an event of thought.

It is in this sense that dramatization is a critical method. In the previous chapter, we characterized critical methods as those that draw epistemological inspiration, albeit often implicitly, from Marx's eleventh thesis on Feuerbach: 'philosophers have only interpreted the world, in various ways, the point is to change it' (McLellan, 2000, 173). That is, critical methods agree that knowledge regarding the social and political world, in particular, will only emerge in the process of transforming society and politics. In certain variants of Marxism, this takes the form of the revolutionary upheaval of capitalism by the universal class, the proletarians. In certain variants of feminism, this requires the overthrow of patriarchy in order for women to be able to know what it is even possible to think as a woman. In Deleuze and Guattari's version of a critical method, we can know the social and political world by dramatizing the concepts that constitute it in the act of making a significant difference to thought, creating an event.

This may not seem a very fruitful method from a critical point of view on the two grounds mentioned earlier; first, on the grounds that it appears woefully caught up in the game of philosophical invention and, secondly, on the grounds that it seems divested of all real sense of political engagement with a specific form of oppression. These are both charges that have been laid at the door of Deleuze and Guattari and it is important to address them. What's more, however, any critical method worth its salt must also be able to justify itself against other methods – and it is with this discussion that we close this chapter.

The politics of dramatization

Many commentators sympathetic to the philosophical rigours of Deleuze and Guattari's system have baulked at the apparent lack of critical bite it would seem to entail (Badiou and Žižek are but the two most prominent representatives of this at present). There is a general concern that they are engaged in what Rèe (1995) dismissively called 'philosophy for philosophy's sake': that the affirmation of dramatic re-conceptualizations is merely ivory-tower posturing, impotent in the face of real political challenges. We cannot go into all the issues these charges bring here, though we have discussed them elsewhere (MacKenzie, 1997; 2004; Porter, 2006; 2009). For now, our focus must be on clarifying further what is meant by a concept, by the dramatization of concepts, and by making an event of thought.

One way of neatly summarizing the previous two sections is to say that a concept is a multiplicity that surveys an event. Every concept already has more than one component to it. The concept of the state, for example, has numerous components including territory, sovereignty, a people, authority and such like. Equally, each of these concepts has multiple components. That said, concepts do not have infinite component parts because every concept must leave out other concepts in order to define itself. So a concept is 'a finite multiplicity', to use Deleuze and Guattari's phrasing from *What is Philosophy?* This is another way of saying that the concept expresses an indeterminate idea that nonetheless requires conceptualizations; this is the two-sided nature of concepts that we discussed above.

To say that each concept surveys an event is therefore to say that it includes multiple elements that express the event. We recall the example of crystallization discussed above. The concept does not represent the actual individuated crystals that have formed (for example, we may say the crystals were beautiful and by this mean that they are particularly luminous, reflective and such like) rather it expresses the event of their formation from out of the ideal solution that itself contained many different potential individuations: of which this particularly beautiful formation is only one. That is to say, concepts (at least 'good concepts' as we will see) describe the process rather than the product because the process has ontological priority over the product that emerges. Similarly with regard to the state: this concept should not, when well used, be taken to represent actually existing political formations, but rather to explain that these formations emerged at all – i.e. that the state is the result of a process that explains the particular qualities that actually existing states have acquired.

The dramatization of concepts, on this view, is the process by which one 'recovers' the events that conditioned their emergence. As we have argued throughout, however, this can only be achieved in light of contemporary conditions. We can only conceptualize the relevance of the concept of the state if we engage thoroughly with how its contemporary forms express the intensive relationships that gave rise to it in the first place. In other words, we must approach the state as a form still in process, even when it appears to have acquired a sedentary and fixed nature. In much used Deleuze parlance, we must ask what the state is *becoming* rather than what it is: 'is the state still relevant?' rather than 'what is the state?' As we discussed in the previous chapter, Guattari was well aware (more so than Deleuze perhaps) that asking questions such as these was an intrinsically political endeavour. As Guattari was fond of saying, it is the impertinence of such questions, all too readily policed and excluded from public discourse, that reminds us that micropolitical activity must begin in the nursery; that is, it must begin with the naïve and simple questions of those who have not yet been told to 'know better'. In other words, there is a politics to the questions one asks and dramatization is a method that forces us to ask political questions.

Of course, it might be argued that, in moving from the ivory-tower to the nursery, the real site of political contestation – namely the street – remains occluded. However, the clarification of what a concept is, and how one dramatizes it, has made no reference to the fact that it must be philosophers (in our present world, this seems to mean state-funded academics, although this is changing) that engage in this process. On the contrary, philosophers of the paid-up variety are typically those that engage in well-worn and well-defended processes of de-dramatization; that is, in their attempts to proclaim the naturalness of certain concepts against others. In Deleuze and Guattari's terminology, they are the idealists who seek to bridge the unbridgeable distance between the concept and the plane (or idea) that it expresses by arguing that *this* concept *really* conveys what is meant by the idea. Equally, we can say that the dramatization of concepts is as likely, and perhaps more likely, to occur on the streets as it is in the ivory-towers or the nursery. There is nothing in being a professional philosopher that privileges these individuals in the use and dramatization of concepts. Indeed, Deleuze and Guattari are adamant that the philosopher is the concept's friend and these friends can be found in every walk of life – walking the streets as well as the quad.

The crucial requirement for being the friend of the concept, however, is that one recognizes it for the intensity it is, that one does not deaden concepts by running down rabbit holes after their essence but keeps them alive by always using them in forceful and pertinent ways. Being the friend of the concept in this sense means being one who is always willing to make an event of thought. As we recall from *What is Philosophy?*, the philosopher is the one who creates concepts and to create concepts means to create events. What is more, the philosopher need not be an individual; it could just as easily be a pair, a group or social movement. Any movement, for example, spurred to respond to an event by creating a new way of articulating their existence, a new concept (which can just as readily be a new version of an established concept), is a philosopher (Svirsky, 2010 contains many interesting examples of this general claim). If this philosopher then develops the perspective that the concept expresses without undermining the difference between the concept and the significant event from which it has resulted, then this philosopher is dramatizing the world that we inhabit by making an event in thought that will resonate throughout all other thoughts – at least potentially. That said, this does not imply that the philosopher will or must call everyone under the banner of this new image of thought. Indeed, the concept–idea–event relationship is one of mutual conditioning and indeterminacy and any attempt to do so would be to occlude the internally problematic nature of those relationships. In sum, we can say that all critical methods espouse creative intervention, but only dramatization maintains that creativity because of the problematic nature of the idea it seeks to express.

But how does this help us think about how we access the political? To state it as clearly as possible: every conceptualization of the elements of political reality is conditioned by an idea of the political, just as every idea of the political is conditioned by our conceptualizations of everyday politics. If we change one side of this two-sided ontology in a significant way, and we do so as individuals asking pertinent questions in seminars or nurseries or as groups taking to the streets in the name of new form of existence, then we bring an event to thought that illuminates our understanding of the political world. In political theory, dramatization as method requires that we stage new relations within and between the concepts that animate politics in order to express the indeterminate, yet endlessly provocative, nature of the idea of the political. This complex set of relations can be set in motion when we forsake questions that look for the essence of the concepts that we use (what is 'X'?), and instead ask questions about the force or power of concepts in particular circumstances – such as 'how do I play the "knight of faith", the "proletarian"?'; 'how useful is the concept of the state to contemporary political life?'; 'does rationality have any force when we think about human relationships?'; 'to what extent is justice applicable to the family?', and so on. The results of such questions, to the extent that they do not return to questions of essence, are always a provocation to political thought because they condition concepts that are (potentially, at least) expressive of the idea of the political. And, after all, isn't that what political theory is all about?

Part II

4
Language and the Method of Dramatization

In Part One of the book we situated Deleuze and Guattari's work in a political theory context (chapter one), then traced the emergence, consolidation and continuing importance of dramatization as a critical method (chapter two), before exploring the ontological claims that sustain this method as such (chapter three). As we have already indicated, in this second half of the book we are motivated by two general concerns going forward. First, we want to address head-on, so to speak, some of the ways in which the method of dramatization can be put to work. Second, to foresee and tackle problems with the method as they arise in the context of our putting it to work. The narrative that will emerge across chapters four, five and six will, we hope, become clear (though not without some complication) and it can be anticipated with the following brief sketch.

In this fourth chapter we will be specifically concerned to draw out some ways of thinking about how the method of dramatization can be put to work in relation to language. One of key themes that will emerge later in the chapter is Deleuze and Guattari's modernism, or, what we will come to call the problem of their modernism. It will be recalled (chapter two) that we raised a couple of problems against Deleuze and Guattari's method as it particularly related to modernism. On the one hand, we registered a worry about the splitting up of knowledge into separate domains (about the way Deleuze and Guattari separate out or differentiate the domains of art, science and philosophy in *What is Philosophy?*). And, on the other hand, there was concern about whether or not the re-emergence of dramatization, through the discussion of the conceptual personae in their final collaborative work, amounted to a depoliticizing move whereby their method comes to sit in a curiously abstract relationship to politics. It is important to see how these problems are connected. For one of the dangers of insisting on a distinction between different domains of knowledge is that we, despite our best efforts and against protestations to the contrary, fall into the trap of then privileging one domain over the others (think, for example, of the naturalism or scientism of the political scientist as discussed in chapter two). These are problems that we will again take up, addressing them implicitly and explicitly across all the three chapters in question. So, after establishing the problem of Deleuze and Guattari's modernism in relation to their work on language and linguistics (chapter four), we then pursue this in a more detailed fashion through a discussion of Jacques Rancière's and Alain Badiou's critique of the modernism they find in Deleuze's cinema books (chapter five), a discussion which then opens up the possibility of critically engaging with Deleuze and Guattari's general aesthetics in *What is Philosophy?* (chapter six). And what we shall emerge in these final chapters (among other things) is a clear question mark being put against Deleuze and Guattari's argument that art and philosophy exist in a separate, but equal, relation. Indeed, it is both the implicit and explicit contention of critics like Rancière and Badiou that Deleuze (and Guattari) privilege philosophy over art in a way that depoliticizes the potential of the latter; that is, the politics of aesthetics in Deleuze and Guattari becomes the particular property of a philosophical meta-language that determines, and thereby nullifies, it in advance.

Now, although we concede that the modernist problem identified by Rancière and Badiou will indeed prove to be stubbornly persistent and problematic, we nonetheless want to counter the blanket claim that Deleuze and Guattari's work generally, or the method of dramatization in particular, is fatally lacking in critical bite and political efficacy. In one sense, we will simply show, as we have said, how the method can be put to work, or directed to practical engagements whose political efficacy the reader can evaluate as they are unfolded across the book as a totality. So whether this is showing how Deleuze and Guattari engage in conceptual debates familiar to the political philosopher (for example, the concept of freedom as discussed in chapter one), or how their own new lexicon of political-philosophical concepts can be used as a resource to critically engage social and political formations (for example, below, in this chapter, we will use their concept of the 'slogan' to think about contemporary Belfast as a 'post-conflict' city), or, finally, how aesthetic forms are themselves invested with an autonomy to think, and think politically (a key theme in Deleuze's cinema books to be discussed in the next chapter), the intuition in each case relates back to our opening proposition of chapter one – namely that Deleuze and Guattari are political philosophers and should be read as such.

With the above general sketch of chapters four, five and six in place, let us now turn more particularly to Deleuze and Guattari's thinking on language, and its relation to the method of dramatization. One of the key gestures or practical moves that we want to make in this context is to show that Deleuze and Guattari are dramatists who work in the medium of language: we want to show how they, as writers, dramatize by performing or using language in particular ways. Before we begin to try to make this practical move, it is perhaps worth briefly mentioning that it importantly implies that Deleuze and Guattari's work should be given its due as a philosophy of language, that what they say about language and how they use it immediately enters into a critical, and potentially productive, relationship with other key figures and movements in the philosophy of language, or even contemporary linguistics. James Williams, for instance, is his impressive book on Deleuze's *Logic of Sense* shows incredible 'pedagogic flair', to quote Jean-Jacques Lecercle, in establishing a number of potentially fruitful lines of enquiry, connecting up, as he does, Deleuze's work and some pressing problems in contemporary philosophy of language (Williams, 2008). Moreover, Lecercle has been a longstanding and energetic champion of Deleuze and Guattari's work in this field, not only in emphasizing their importance to a thorough rethinking of language philosophy but also in suggesting how they can be used to recast some of the problematic methodological assumptions that inform contemporary programmes of research in linguistics (Lecercle 2006; 2002; 1999a; 1994; 1990; 1985).

Humour

If the method of dramatization is a method that aims to determine the dynamic nature of concepts (political or otherwise) by bringing them to life, then language is a key medium through which Deleuze and Guattari engage in the *practice* of dramatizing as such. Immediately, we can think of this simply as the act of writing, or at least as a potential implied by the act of writing. So a key question immediately presents itself: how do Deleuze and Guattari write? It is necessary to think of the style or form of their writing as fundamental to the architecture of their argument rather than as a flowery, but essentially contingent, add-on. So, if we read Deleuze and Guattari and we are moved, say to smile or laugh, it is essential that we understand this effect as something which productively functions in the argument we are being confronted with;

that the style or form of humour has a significant philosophical function. In the nineteenth series of *Logic of Sense*, Deleuze describes the philosophical importance of humour in the following passage:

> every time we will be asked... "what is Beauty, Justice, Man" we will respond by designating a body, by indicating a object which can be imitated or even consumed, and by delivering, if necessary, a blow to the staff (the staff being the instrument of every possible designation). Diogenes the Cynic answers Plato's definition of man as a biped and featherless animal by bringing forth a plucked fowl. And to the person who asks "what is philosophy?" Diogenes responds by carrying about a cod on the end of a string. The fish is indeed the most oral of animals; it poses the problem of muteness, of consumability, and of the consonant in the wet/palatalized elements – in short, the problem of language. (Deleuze, 1990, 135)

This passage warrants close attention, not simply for its meaning, what is signifies or designates, but also for its potential effects on the reader, dramatic effects. Williams importantly emphasizes how Deleuze's sentences in *Logic of Sense* come in a kind of 'multi-dimensional' form, reflecting a 'rich and chaotic style' which aims not at a 'single meaning or content' but allows for a 'multiple mixture of modes, meanings, physical hooks and emotional connections' (Williams, 2008, 20). In one sense, we find Deleuze making a particular and rather direct claim about the philosophical value and use of posing certain kinds of questions. And what he says here very much connects to a felt sense that questions that come in the form of 'what is...' are the wrong kind of question. Remember (from chapter three) how Deleuze insisted that questions framed by way of the 'what' must give way to questions like those we saw him pose in his defence of Doctorat d'Etat; namely, questions like 'How? How much? Where and when? In which case?' (Deleuze, 2004, 95–96; see also Deleuze, 1994, 246). Against the abstraction of the 'what' we find Deleuze, as he says, descending to bodies, objects, things, which when encountered throw the question of the 'what' (and indeed its solution or answer) up in the air. This is precisely what Deleuze means by humour, the philosophical importance of humour; it is an art of 'descent' (Deleuze, 1990, 135).

Hence the singular importance of Diogenes to Deleuze; Diogenes' dissenting response descends critically on the Platonic question and answer (question: 'what is man?' answer: 'man is a featherless biped!'), and can, for example, work on readers by dramatizing and bringing into sharp relief the feeling that real care and humility needs to be shown by anyone who would assume responsibility for philosophical instruction or, for that matter, any kind of learning. Indeed, for us, as teachers (we flatter ourselves, of course) in a university setting it is hard not to respond to this passage in *Logic of Sense* without some emotion or felt sense that our students, like Diogenes, may desire to perform their own acts of humorous sabotage in order to render problematic our, often, rather odd, infuriating and obtuse locutions and ways of thinking and teaching. And, of course, our students (if we can create the right environment) do this all the time. One example will suffice to illustrate the point (and yes this really happened).

Picture the scene; an earnest lecturer is delivering a lecture on Adorno and falls into a rather long-winded, inattentive and digressive rumination about 'pseudo-individuation'. Struggling to retain focus and cogency, and seeing the students starting to drift off, our lecturer begins to fall back into cliché and standardized remarks about 'standardization', about the world being highly 'administered' and 'conceptually shot-through with the logic of the commodity form' etc. Now, wind the clock forward; in the seminar the next week, the students are asked to present papers discussing how and where we may see evidence of 'pseudo-individuation' operating in political or other institutions, or indeed in the broader culture. Two students responded not by presenting a paper, but, in effect, by doing a performance; making their earnest lecturer the butt of a rather clever joke. One student played the lecturer (with relevant tics, non-verbals, intonations, and endless repetition of the same pop-culture references), while the other played the student body, but a student body that didn't just passively sit and silently think about the silliness of their situation, but one which started to say out loud things like: 'oh God, not another snide comment about the "pseudo-individuation" of IKEA products'; or 'here we go again with vague and rather baseless remarks about the genius of New Order's first three albums'; or 'doesn't it occur to him that making those hand gestures, or fiddling with his watch like that, or saying "apropos", is incredibly off-putting, distracting and irritating...'.

The gesture the students were making, of course, was one of humorously descending on their lecturer to show the very standardized and repetitive form in which the concept of 'pseudo-individuation' was discussed. Focusing less on the content of what was said in the lecture and more on the *form* of its delivery (again the tics, non-verbals, intonations, the pop-culture references) they brought into sharp relief their own experience of 'pseudo-individuation' in the institution where they found themselves – the university. In this regard, our students are proper Deleuzeans, at least in the sense that the humorous *form* of their dramatization or expression was at once very much part of the architecture of their argument. Yes, what they did was funny in and of itself (and yes, there was perhaps an element of wanting to simply take the piss), but, and this is a crucial point, the humour played a particular role in their learning and in the learning of all in the class (even, or especially, the lecturer). Humour plays a role in learning, for Deleuze, precisely because it creates an important felt sense that what often passes for supposedly informed or rational instruction (in this case, our lecturer's ruminations about 'pseudo-individuation') has limited sense, that it remains problematic in some way. There is therefore wisdom to be found when one embarks on 'this adventure of humour' (Deleuze, 1990, 136).

This takes us back again to the passage above. For, as we can see, Deleuze is not simply making an argument for the philosophical importance of humour by way of a supposedly informed and rational instruction; *he is dramatizing or bringing to life an argument precisely through a form of writing that is humorous.* Now, of course, Deleuze is informed and his argument has a rational form to it. Clearly, he draws on Diogenes the Cynic (and indeed elsewhere on the Stoics and elements of Buddhism) to develop a concept of humour that critically descends on the Platonic form of the philosophical question ('what is "X"?'). But this is only one dimension as his sentences also carry with them a potential emotional connection and resonance (for example, the teacher who learns to learn from her/his clever and humorous students) and, even, puzzlement and confusion. For Deleuze's *Logic of Sense* (as anyone who has ever picked up the book will readily testify) often puzzles and confuses. But this experience of puzzlement and confusion can be productive. Let us consider again the last two sentences of the passage. In the penultimate sentence Deleuze says that; 'to the person who asks "what is philosophy?" Diogenes responds by carrying about a cod on the end of a string'. Now, what, on earth, are we supposed to do with this information? Why a cod? Is it a cod? Deleuze continues and concludes in the final sentence: 'The fish is indeed the most oral of animals; it poses the problem of muteness, of consumability, and of the consonant in the wet/palatalized elements – in short, the problem of language'.

The productive aspect of the potential confusion caused by Deleuze's final sentence here is not to be found in some declarative or propositional resolution (for instance, 'Deleuze's reference to the cod means X!'), but in the series of concepts we are forced to think about in relation to the body or object of our confusion – namely the 'cod' (that is, 'orality', 'consumption', 'muteness' and so on) – and a sustained reading of *Logic of Sense* would show where these concepts are taken up in a variety of ways, helping Deleuze make some sense of what he calls the 'problem of language'. So we might be moved, in our confusion, to look at Deleuze's arguments in the twenty-seventh series on 'orality', or to connect the concept of 'orality' to 'consumption', as Deleuze does, for instance, in his discussion of Louis Wolfson in the thirteenth series (Deleuze, 1990, 186 & 84–85). What is important in this context is the creation of a felt sense in the reader that we must survey, connect up, and give some consistency to a series of related concepts; that, more generally put, we are moved, through humour, puzzlement, confusion, to engage with concepts.

From humour to slogans

But there is confusion and there is confusion. There is the confusion that provokes and moves us to try to think and there is the confusion that feeds off wilful obstinacy and a determination to be unimpressed: the confusion of the sceptic. There is no doubt that Deleuze's *Logic of Sense* is a text that we could read with obstinacy, with scepticism, with a determination to be unimpressed. But this is an unproductive reading, a humourless reading. In *Kafka*, Deleuze and Guattari insist on the importance of reading Kafka with a sense of humour and with a critical sensitivity to how his humour is fundamental to his politics; that is, how his humour operates in the creation of certain political concepts. As Deleuze and Guattari say: 'only two principles are necessary to accord with Kafka. He is an author who laughs with a profound joy, a *joie de vivre*, in spite of, or because of, his own clownish declarations that he offers like a trap or a circus. And from one end to the other, he is a political author' (Deleuze and Guattari, 1986, 41). The compliment that Deleuze and Guattari pay to Kafka can also be paid to Deleuze and Guattari themselves. For like Kafka, they are authors who use humour in the creation of their political concepts. A good example of this is the concept of the *slogan* that they develop in the fourth plateau of *A Thousand Plateaus*, 'the postulates of linguistics' (Deleuze and Guattari, 1988, 75–110).

Now, rather than try to engage directly with the concept of the 'slogan' at this point, it is perhaps better to introduce it more slowly, indirectly and by way of a source that might seem rather odd in the first instance. The following passage is taken from a conversation or interview Deleuze had with Christian Deschamps, Didier Eribon and Robert Maggiori around the time of the publication of *A Thousand Plateaus*. At one point, Maggiori tentatively suggests to Deleuze that his and Guattari's reflections on language and linguistics in *A Thousand Plateaus* seem to have a conceptual or philosophical prominence comparable to that of their treatment of psychoanalysis in *Anti-Oedipus*. Consider Deleuze's response:

> I don't think that linguistics is fundamental. Maybe Felix, if he were here, would disagree. But then Felix has traced a development that points towards a transformation of linguistics: initially it was phonological, then it was semantic and syntactic, but it's turning more and more into pragmatics. Pragmatics (dealing with the circumstances of language-use, with events and acts) was long considered the "rubbish dump" of linguistics, but it's now becoming more and more important: language is coming to be seen as an activity, so the abstract units and constants of language-use are becoming less and less important. It's a good thing, this current direction of research, precisely because it makes possible convergences and collaborations between novelists, linguists, philosophers, "vocalists"... ("vocalists" are what I call anyone doing research into sound or the voice in fields as varied as theatre, song, cinema, audio-visual media ...). The potential here is enormous... I don't think we, for our part, are particularly competent to pronounce on linguistics. But then competence is itself a rather unclear notion in linguistics.... (Deleuze, 1995, 28–9)

This is a fascinating passage of talk (and that it is talk is significant, as we shall see in a moment) and there is much to detain us here. Deleuze begins the passage by saying 'I don't think that linguistics is fundamental' and ends it declaring that he and Guattari are not 'particularly competent to pronounce on linguistics'. Again, there is a particular Deleuzean sense of humour in evidence here. And this humour is very much connected to the idea of talk, of speech-action, of performing something in the act of saying something. It makes very little sense to simply read Deleuze's remarks in terms of their designative function ('linguistics is not fundamental!'; 'Guattari and I are not competent to pronounce on linguistics'). Rather it is more productive to read Deleuze's remarks for their dramatic and humorous effects, as 'smiling provocations' (Williams, 2008, 21). So why might we smile, and why might we be provoked by Deleuze's words in this context? We may form a wry smile because a familiarity with Deleuze and Guattari's work on linguistics in *A Thousand Plateaus* immediately suggests that Deleuze's declaration of ignorance is itself a humorous provocation. Immediately, we are provoked to read this fragment of talk against the backcloth of some of the key claims they make in the fourth plateau. Let us try to unpack this in more detail.

When Deleuze says 'I don't think that linguistics is fundamental', he is not making a particular value judgement about the importance of the study of language, but a broader political point about how the disciplinary borders of linguistics are policed. These disciplinary boundaries are precisely the 'postulates of linguistics' that Deleuze and Guattari seek to challenge in plateau four (See Lecercle, 2006; 2002; 1999a). This can explain why Deleuze immediately qualifies his first sentence with the suggestion that 'Maybe Felix, if he were here, would disagree', pointing generously to Guattari's influence and work in the field and in their developing conception of 'pragmatics' (Lecercle, 2002, 51). For the concept of 'pragmatics', as Deleuze says, should not be seen as the 'rubbish dump' of linguistics, but rather as fundamentally important to all aspects of language study. Indeed, Deleuze and Guattari insist in plateau four that the student of language should (indeed needs) to practice a form of pragmatics, where 'pragmatics' traces the internal or intrinsic relations between speech and action: for example, when a promise of love is at once the action of making a promise (Deleuze and Guattari, 1988, 77). Or, put more strongly still, Deleuze and Guattari rather provocatively assert that pragmatics is fundamental not only to the study of language-use in speech action, but is crucial for understanding the other branches or fields of what is sometimes called 'linguistic science': for instance, semantics, syntactics, phonematics and so on. In this respect, pragmatics, for Deleuze and Guattari, 'becomes the presupposition behind all other dimensions and insinuates itself into everything' (Deleuze and Guattari, 1988, 77).

This brings us back again neatly to Deleuze's remarks about competence, how the concept of 'competence' functions in linguistics. There is no doubt that he has Chomsky, and the various research programmes influenced by Chomskyian linguistics, in mind. For declaring his and Guattari's lack of competence in linguistics is a humorous provocation as soon as we realize that it is a well-thought out implication of the pragmatic turn that Deleuze and Guattari think is necessary for the student of language. The final sentence in the passage above is the obvious clincher, should we be in any doubt about the penultimate one. To repeat: 'I don't think we, for our part, are particularly competent to pronounce on linguistics. But then competence is itself a rather unclear notion in linguistics'. The reason that competence is a 'rather unclear notion' is precisely because it functions as part of a dualism that is endlessly complicated by the variations that are set in motion by speech action. As is well known, Chomsky draws an important distinction between competence and what he calls performance. Where 'performance' may be thought of as the extrinsic, individual and context-specific use of pre-given deep syntactic structure or language system, 'competence' is best seen more as an 'innate' faculty the language-user has for creatively generating new forms of syntax in accordance with this deep or pre-given systematicity or structure. Against Chomsky, Deleuze and Guattari argue that it is impossible to maintain a distinction between competence and performance as the systematicity or constancy of the former (as reflective of a deep syntactic structure) can no longer be assumed independently of the latter. Put simply, speech action should not be seen as the extrinsic, individual or context-specific use of the resources always-already available in a deep syntactic structure, but syntax itself needs to be accounted for by the way it is actualized and continually renewed in and through speech action. The 'meaning and syntax of language can no longer be defined independently of the speech acts they presuppose' (Deleuze and Guattari, 1988, 77).

Speech action sets language in motion, a 'continuous variation', that renders problematic what Deleuze describes in passing in the passage above as 'abstract units and constants of language-use' (read: constants like Chomsky's 'competence' or, say, Saussure's notion of 'langue' as a structure or system independent of 'parole'). The stress on constancy or pre-given structures in language, for Deleuze, is 'becoming less and less important' the more and more 'pragmatics' inspires us to view language as an open system of continual variation and, in this respect, it can converge with research work undertaken by 'vocalists' in other fields of enquiry; that is 'anyone doing research into sound or the voice in fields as varied as theatre, song, cinema, audio-visual media...'. For us, this is an extremely suggestive remark as it reinforces the importance of the performative aspect of language-use, giving readers a license to think of Deleuze and Guattari's language-use as a dramatizing, varying, modulating, vocalism. Deleuze and Guattari can indeed be viewed as vocalists, or their writing can be thought to imply a vocalism, where 'vocalism' connects to the idea that the variations, modulations and movements in language issue from the medium itself, and not just simply from the extrinsic or particular context of their enunciation. In this way, Deleuze and Guattari offer a form of 'pragmatics' that is rather interesting and provocative. It is a pragmatics that insists, inevitably, on the importance of performance in language, or the use of language in speech action, while simultaneously retaining the idea that language is characterized by a kind of intrinsic or immanent movement that issues from the medium itself. In this sense, we can begin to refer to Deleuze and Guattari's pragmatics in *A Thousand Plateaus* as a *modernist pragmatics*.

Of course, such labels mean precisely nothing unless and until we begin to put them to work. At one point in plateau four, Deleuze and Guattari pose the question of how to conceptualize the immanent and continuous variation of language quite directly, and their answer is worth considering at length. Let us lay out the quote first:

> How can we conceptualize this continuous variation at work within a language...? In the course of a single day, an individual repeatedly passes from language to language. He successively speaks as "father to son" and as a boss; to his lover, he speaks an infantilized language; while sleeping he is plunged into an oniric discourse, then abruptly returns to a professional language when the telephone rings. It will be objected that these variations are extrinsic, that it is still the same language. But that is to prejudge the question. First, it is not certain that the phonology is the same, nor the syntax, nor the semantics. Second, the whole question is whether this supposedly identical language is defined by invariants or...by the line of continuous variation running through it.... Take as an example "I swear!" It is a different statement depending on whether it is said by a child to her father, by a man in love to his loved one, or a witness before the court.... Once again, there is no reason to say that the variables are merely situational, and that the statement remains constant in principle. Not only are there as many statements as there are effectuations, but all of the statements are present in the effectuation of one among them, so that the line of variation is virtual.... To place the statement in continual variation is to send it through all prosodic, semantic, syntactical and phonological variables that can affect it.... This is the standpoint of pragmatics, but a pragmatics internal to language, immanent, including variations of linguistic elements of all kinds. (Deleuze and Guattari, 1988, 94)

As we can see, the key claim being made concerning the continual and immanent variability of language is glossed by Deleuze and Guattari with reference to a couple of examples or, better still, imagined scenarios. First, we have an individual going about his daily business, engaging in various forms of speech action (as a father, boss, lover and dreamer...). Second, we have a particular statement ("I swear!") operationalized across a variety of situations (father–daughter, lover–loved one, witness–court...). In both cases, Deleuze and Guattari insist that the variations running through these forms of language-use are poorly understood if we simply reduce them to the situation or actual context of operation. The statement, speech action, or language as such, has two coexisting sides: an actual side and a virtual side (and we can start to see how the two-fold ontology of the virtual and actual from Deleuze's *Difference and Repetition*, discussed in chapter three, subsequently gets operationalized or re-engineered in Deleuze and Guattari's later collaborative work). Thinking the 'actual' in relation to language, we can say it connects to the particular situational or contextual moment of its operation, while the virtual we can think of as a potential 'continuum or medium' of language as such; that is, a potential for variation that is, in principle, 'without beginning or end' (Deleuze and Guattari, 1988, 94). So we are beginning to bring into view a problem that is peculiar to Deleuze and Guattari's pragmatics. The key question, then, is this: how can we account for the two-sided nature of language, for its performance or use in actual situations and contexts, but also the virtual line of continuous variation that runs through it?

Posing the problem in this way allows us, finally, to focus explicitly on Deleuze and Guattari's notion of the slogan. Or, better still, it is through an engagement with the concept of the slogan that we can make fuller sense of their claim about the two-sided nature of language. How so? We will use the rest of the chapter to work through an example that will, hopefully, do the necessary work for us. Although there are many slogans that one could lift from Deleuze and Guattari's remarks in plateau four, and indeed from elsewhere in their writings, we have our own example in mind. The slogan is: *Belfast is a post-conflict city!*

Belfast is a post-conflict city!

The importance of slogans or, what can also be called, 'order-words' are emphasized time and again by Deleuze and Guattari in plateau four of *A Thousand Plateaus*. Put simply, they argue that any critical-political analysis of language must proceed on the basis that language operates through the issuing of slogans or order-words. That is to say, the functioning of order-words or slogans is 'co-extensive' with the operation of language as such. Unsurprisingly, Deleuze and Guattari make this argument in a typically formalist, humorous and dramatic fashion; that is, initially framing it by way of a slogan. They say, or sloganize as follows; 'Language is made not to be believed but to be obeyed, and to compel obedience' (Deleuze and Guattari, 1988, 76). How, then, do slogans do their work? How do they order things, compel obedience?

The slogan that 'Belfast is a post-conflict city!' does important work in the particular social formation to which it is attributed by operating as a promise. That is to say, the idea of Belfast as a 'post-conflict' city is constituted in and through the promise that we are seeing in Northern Ireland the emergence of a public sphere or an experience of public life that is no longer primarily shaped by the antagonisms generated by politically motivated violence; a promise of 'peace' and 'prosperity' (these have become the two key signifiers). It is worth pointing out that this slogan has come in a number of social-cultural forms or genres; it has a multi-media grammar. The image of Belfast as a post-conflict city has, since the Good Friday Agreement in 1998, been operative in commercial discourses relating to property development and urban regeneration, in local news media, television drama, film, architecture and so on (See McLaughlin and Baker, 2010; Dewesbury and Porter 2010). In order to best understand the political or ordering function that this image of the city performs, it is necessary to think in *normative* terms; that is, to see the slogan as gesturing in the direction of an ideal towards which the city must move, rather than as a description of an actually existing formation. It is certainly not the case that Belfast is a city completely at peace with itself, that sectarian antagonism is a thing of the past. Indeed, it is clear that many of the citizens of Belfast live in a city still deeply divided and segregated on ethno-political or sectarian lines (Shirlow and Murtagh 2006).

If the slogan that Belfast is a post-conflict city tends toward a normative ideal, it does not necessarily follow that its ordering function is of limited significance. The slogan does not simply operate on the basis of facts, or in accordance with a logic of the true, but, rather, on the basis of its appropriateness or, as Althusser might have said, its 'correctness' in its adjustment to the 'conjuncture' (Althusser, 1997). From a Deleuze–Guattarian perspective, we can understand the critical purchase that any given slogan may have in the social-political formation through its operation in, what they call, 'collective assemblages of enunciation'. For Deleuze and Guattari, statements, slogans, language-use in actual social-political situations, implies collective assemblages. As they say: 'the statement is individuated, and the enunciation subjectified, only to the extent that an impersonal collective assemblage requires it and determines it to be so' (Deleuze and Guattari, 1988, 80). We can think of the collective assemblages in a number of ways; for example, as cli-chés, an easy-to-hand reserve of ready-made expressions and thoughts that we may want to quickly draw on in regulating, patterning or order-ing our world. Think about the clichés that we constantly fall back on to regulate social situations and pattern social interaction (for instance, the clichés that we repeat as parents to our children, the clichés of the teacher, the clichéd response of the bored student, the clichés that per-meate our everyday talk with acquaintances, friends, colleagues and so on). Clichés belong to no one, properly speaking, and are impersonal in that sense. They issue from no one and operate on the basis of 'hearsay' or as a 'free indirect discourse' (Deleuze and Guattari, 1988, 80).

The slogan that Belfast is a post-conflict city has become something of a cliché in the Deleuze–Guattarian sense, implying, as it does, a col-lective assemblage that has implicated itself in the social formation as a series of regulated and patterned actions; as prior orderings or 'order-words', if you like. What are these regulated and patterned actions, these orderings? Well, one of the most crucial points to note here is that the normative promise of the post-conflict city permits, indeed impera-tively commands, us to think the political in Belfast, and in Northern Ireland more generally, in a particular way. That is to say, the prom-ise of 'peace' and 'prosperity' lends itself to a more technocratic and supposedly post-ideological (read: post-sectarian) politics concerned with 'normalization' and 'development'. Had we a taste for rather inel-egant phrasing, we could call this a *moralizing politics of economic-socio-political development*. What we are suggesting with this phrasing is that economic, social and political development has come together to form a normatively articulated conjunction in 'post-conflict' Belfast, a new moral economy in which it becomes 'appropriate' or 'correct' to view those agents capable of delivering such 'development' (for example, multi-national companies investing locally, or indeed local property developers and assorted entrepreneurs doing so) as 'moral' actors as such (see Dewesbury and Porter, 2010; Porter, 2009).

The imperative to see Belfast as a post-conflict city implies that we view economic and social development as imperative, which implies that the support of agents capable of delivering such development is imperative, which implies that their actions in the developing economy are seen as good, which implies, of course, that critical scrutiny of their actions becomes difficult to sustain in a social formation where the moral compass is set in accordance with a form of technocratic ration-ality summed up by the oft-repeated imperative or infinitive verb – 'to develop', 'to develop', 'to develop'. What we mean by saying all this, of course, is that the imperatives or orders at play in the slogan that Belfast is a post-conflict city operate implicitly within it and connect to social formation in an immediate way. And all of these implicit orders or imperatives make up the collective assemblage in and through which the slogan begins to make sense and take on social-political significance. So just because a slogan is not explicitly marked by an imperative or order, this should not detract us from the militarism of its operation. As Deleuze and Guattari put it, the orders or imperatives that flow through language 'do not flow from primary significations or result from information: an order always and already concerns prior orders...'(Deleuze and Guattari, 1988, 75).

Slogans are handed down to us, they order things, compel obedience, shaping our mode of subjectivity accordingly. For example, in the new Belfast of 'peace' and 'prosperity' a domesticated and consumptive mode of subjectivity has become incredibly important to the 'development' and 'normalization' of the city (McLaughlin and Baker, 2010). In other words, there has been an arrangement of various economic and cultural technologies that have acted on subjects, shifting focus away from what we could call 'politicized subjects' (read; 'sectarian subjects') to 'consumer-subjects' or, to steal Paul Langley's term, 'investor-subjects' who are concerned to understand themselves, and evaluate their own behaviour, on the basis of risk and reward in a social formation increasingly shaped by logics of financialization (Langley, 2007).

Clearly, we can view all of these developments from the point of view of the 'actual'; that is, in terms of the operation of the slogan in the specific context of its enunciation. But: what about the 'virtual' side of the slogan or language? Here things get a bit more complicated, perhaps even counter-intuitive. For not only can order-words or slogans get actualized in and through social formations or collective assemblages, they can also effect what Deleuze and Guattari call the 'incorporeal transformations current in a given society and attributed to the bodies of that society' (Deleuze and Guattari, 1988, 80). We can think of these 'incorporeal transformations' very much in connection to the virtual 'continuum or medium' of language as such. Deleuze and Guattari offer the following examples of 'incorporeal transformations':

> Peace and war are states or interminglings of very different kinds of bodies, but the declaration of a general mobilization expresses an instantaneous and incorporeal transformation of bodies.... Love is an intermingling of bodies that can be represented by a heart with an arrow through it ... but the declaration "I love you" expresses

a noncorporeal attribute of bodies.... Eating bread and drinking wine are interminglings of bodies; communing with Christ is also an intermingling of bodies.... But the transformation of the body of the bread and the wine into the body and the blood of Christ is the pure expressed of a statement attributed to the bodies. In an airplane hijacking, the threat of a hijacker brandishing a revolver is obviously an action.... But the transformation of the passengers into hostages, and of the plane-body into a prison-body, is an instantaneous incorporeal transformation, a "mass media act".... (Deleuze and Guattari, 1988, 81)

So we can see from the examples given by Deleuze and Guattari that language implies an ontological mixture of bodies (the mobilized army, the bread and wine, the lovers, the airplane passengers) but also 'incorporeal attributes', the 'pure expressed of the statement' ('We are now at war!'; 'This is the body of Christ!'; 'I love you!'; 'This is a hijacking!'). The potential that language has to effect these transformations, while clearly actualized in bodies, is a virtual one, something intrinsic or immanent to language as a medium as such (witness Deleuze and Guattari's remarks at the end of the passage about 'mass media acts'). One of the ways to think about this virtual side of language is go back to arguments first developed by Deleuze in *Logic of Sense*. Indeed, seasoned readers of Deleuze will recognize the influence of Stoic logic in the above passage. In *Logic of Sense*, Deleuze famously develops the idea of a kind of incorporeal vapour that, while produced in the actual rough and tumble of bodily mixtures, at once rises above them. As is well known, Deleuze connects this notion of the incorporeal to the concept of the event, a notion that implicitly plays through the above passage and which continues to get worked on by Deleuze and Guattari right through to *What is Philosophy?*

So how can we make sense of this concept of the event? There is much that could be said here (and we will provide a more extensive discussion of the notion of the event in chapter six); but, for the moment, let us begin to dramatize the concept by coming back to our example or slogan; namely, Belfast is a post-conflict city! Thinking back to the collective assemblage or the series of orders or imperatives at play in the slogan, we suggested that they implied a technocratic rationality best summed by the imperative and infinitive verb: 'to develop'. Those familiar with Deleuze's *Logic of Sense* will already recognize in this proposition the potential to view it accordance with the logic of the event and virtual sense. Put simply, Deleuze argues that events and virtual sense are, in principle, expressible in language as infinitive verbs like 'to develop' or, to use his examples, 'to grow', 'to diminish', 'to cut' 'to be cut' (Deleuze, 1990, 4–6 & 184–5). Those readers unfamiliar with Deleuze's *Logic of Sense* may, on the contrary, find what we are saying here utterly baffling and confusing. Please stick with us, read us, and Deleuze, in good humour as we begin to try to make sense of this claim. Perhaps the most helpful thing to say at this juncture is that infinitive verbs like 'to develop' are, in Deleuze's hands, paradoxical (this can explain the bafflement and confusion, at least initially) to the extent that they follow a logic of 'pure becoming' which 'divides itself infinitely in past and future and always eludes the present' (Deleuze, 1990, 5).

So, thinking about the imperative or infinitive verb 'to develop' in the context of the post-conflict city becomes complicated by the sense that it is an imperative that operates within, while simultaneously eluding, the living present. Yes, of course, the imperative 'to develop' (the normative idea that economic and social development of a certain kind is a moral good) lives in the present conjuncture and implies the mixture and movement of bodies (the property developer and multinational investor becoming moral agents of progress, citizens becoming 'investor-subjects' and so on...) but it also, paradoxically, eludes the present as it has both a past and future sense, a virtual sense. One of the reasons that an infinitive like 'to develop' has a virtual sense is because of its virtual potential to enter into relations with other infinitives that can give it a value or significance that is, in principle, open to an infinitely continual variation. For instance, if we say that the slogan or imperative 'to develop' in the post-agreement Belfast of the late 1990s becomes significant – that is, politically or ideologically significant – precisely because it connects to another infinitive such as 'to depoliticize' (say, to view property development, inward investment by multi-nationals and the financialization of everyday modes of consumer/investor subjectivity as necessary progress and, consequently, as beyond any rational political critique), then there is nothing to prevent this relation from changing its significance, or being experienced as a changing relation at another time. Two quick examples will suffice for illustrative purposes.

First, we may look to the Belfast of the 1970s and 1980s, viewing the relation between infinitive verbs such as 'to develop' and 'to depoliticize' in a different way, or as expressing a significance at variance with the Belfast of the late 1990s and early twenty-first century. If one considers, for example, the logics of urban development in the Belfast of the 1970s and 1980s important differences in emphasis are detectable;

a different drama is being played out. In the 1970s and 1980s there was less emphasis and significance placed on using the built environment of the city to project confidence about future 'peace' and 'prosperity' (a tactic more consistently employed in the late 1990s or post-agreement period). Indeed, often the strategy was one of containment and conflict management, of using the developing built environment (say, for example, the building of motorways) to empty, smooth out or depoliticize public spaces that may otherwise have functioned as sites of conflict (Dewesbury and Porter, 2010). Understood in this way, the relation between the infinitives 'to develop' and 'to depoliticize' takes on another sense and significance, which, as we said, is less to do with projecting a new-found confidence in the city and more to do with a desire to police or order public space. Second, we may speculate about a present-becoming-future Belfast in which its citizens begin to negotiate critically the relation between the infinitives 'to develop' and 'to depoliticize', seeing their relation not simply as a sign of unproblematic moral progress toward a supposedly post-ideological or post-sectarian era; but, rather, as evidence to suggest an erosion of active citizenship, or a real lack of much-needed political scrutiny and critique of those supposedly 'moral' agents (multi-nationals, property developers and so on) who have so dramatically developed and reshaped their city. Here the relation between the infinitives 'to develop' and 'to depoliticize' again varies in sense and significance, becoming part of a political negotiation and critique of the present logic of 'development' and 'normalization' as such.

As we have shown throughout the chapter, Deleuze and Guattari can be viewed as dramatists working in the medium of language, as writers who dramatize by performing or using language in particular ways. Whether it is through the use of humour or through the issuing of slogans, Deleuze and Guattari provoke us to see language as a key medium through which to determine and bring to life concepts. From the point of view of their political theory, Deleuze and Guattari's work on language, their pragmatics, is important in getting to grips with how they, as political philosophers, dramatize and constitute political concepts. And, as we suggested earlier, it is also significant in creating a real felt sense that their method of dramatization can be put to work, made to work, by political theorists concerned to critically negotiate actually existing social-political formations. Such, then, is the importance of their pragmatics of the slogan. For the notion of the slogan is not just a key concept in Deleuze and Guattari's political philosophy or lexicon, it is also an extremely useful tool for political theorists like

us who are concerned to negotiate critically a social-political formation such as contemporary Belfast. We offer this example here not to
claim any particular privilege for Belfast as a site for political analysis, or to suggest that this social-political formation is somehow more
amenable to a Deleuze–Guattarian pragmatics than others. Rather, we
offer our thoughts on Belfast as but one potential dramatization among
many others and to underscore the broader methodological point about
the method of dramatization as such; namely, that we come to know,
access, or simply feel the resonance and significance of political concepts like the 'slogan' by playing them out, dramatizing them. In the
previous chapter, when speaking of Deleuze's two-fold ontology of the
virtual and actual, we resorted to the following slogan: *make an event
of thought.* Our hope would be that, cast in light of our discussions in
this chapter, such a slogan now carries with it some further resonance,
efficacy, even provocation.

Before concluding, or by way of conclusion, it is important to come
back to the problem we anticipated in our introductory sketch to this
chapter (and indeed to this second part of the book), and which we
have begun to unfold above. We are, of course, referring to our claim
that Deleuze and Guattari's pragmatics is of a particular type; earlier we
called it a *modernist pragmatics.* By this we meant that they offer a pragmatics that insists, inevitably, on the importance of performance or use
of language in speech action, while simultaneously retaining the idea
that language is characterized by a kind of intrinsic or immanent movement that issues from the medium itself. Now, we tried to account for
this two-sided nature of language through a discussion of the concept of
the slogan: how it implies a collective assemblage in and through which
it is actualized, while nonetheless retaining an incorporeal/evental/vir-
tual sense that is, in principle, open to an infinitely continual variation.
But a problem emerges here concerning a potential charge of linguistic
idealism. That is to say, all this talk about 'incorporeal transformations',
the 'virtual' or 'event' can easily leave the impression that language
is idealistically abstracted from the material, political, conditions that
make its operation possible.

Of course, Deleuze and Guattari want to counter this impression by
emphasizing how the 'incorporeal transformations' effected by slogans
have their material, political, conditions in the collective assemblages in
and through which they assume sense and significance. But, how, then,
does their view differ from a more recognizable pragmatics that simply
insists on an understanding of the political context or circumstances
of enunciation? How can we insist, as Deleuze and Guattari do, on the

capacity or autonomy of language to intervene and directly shape the social-political world, while, at the same time, seemingly explaining incorporeal transformations against the backcloth of collective assemblages? Are collective assemblages just another fancy name for what pragmatists call context or circumstances? At one point in plateau four, Deleuze and Guattari wonder about this and pose the question directly; 'when we use a word as vague as "intervene"... are we not still prey to a kind of idealism in which the slogan instantaneously falls from the sky?' (Deleuze and Guattari, 1988, 81).

Now, this problem, this *modernist problem*, as we want to call it, may well arise, as we have seen, in the context of putting the method of dramatization to work in relation to language. But it is a problem that plays itself out in various ways across Deleuze's and Deleuze and Guattari's work. For example, Deleuze and Guattari's own concern expressed in the quote above, that it may be idealistic or problematic to insist on the capacity or autonomy of a cultural form like language to 'intervene' in and directly shape the social-political world, is one that can be more broadly related to the other cultural or aesthetic forms they engage with, as well as their more general reflections on the art-work. In other words, there is a problem, or a series of problems, that come with investing in the idea that cultural or aesthetic forms have autonomy. We shall see in the next chapter how such problems (the problems of modernism, of the aesthetic autonomy of particular forms or media, of their potentially idealistic abstraction from material-political conditions and so on) get restaged in the context of Deleuze's particular engagement with cinema.

5
Cinema and the Method of Dramatization

This chapter picks up on one of the developing themes of chapter four; namely, the problem of Deleuze and Guattari's modernism. We will initially approach this through a discussion of Deleuze's cinema books and some of the critical literature on *Cinema 1* and *Cinema 2* (Deleuze, 1992; 1989). This might seem an odd way of doing things because it may be thought of as moving us more in the direction of secondary commentary, not to mention potentially editing Guattari out of the picture altogether. But it will prove useful to think about Deleuze's cinema books against the backcloth of some secondary literature (particularly the more caustic and antagonistic commentaries of Jacques Rancière and, to a lesser extent, Alain Badiou) for three important, and related, reasons.

First, the problem of Deleuze's modernism, as expressed in his cinema books, is posed by critics like Rancière and Badiou with great clarity and this will help us bring into much sharper focus some of the problems that follow from raising the issue of modernism in the previous chapter (for example, we will think much more explicitly here about the problem of aesthetic autonomy). Second, the modernist problem that Rancière and Badiou identify in Deleuze's cinema books (essentially, the idea that Deleuze philosophically circumscribes cinema in advance by insisting that it conforms to ready-made concepts that are simply downloaded onto cinematic texts in ways that betray or neutralize any specificity or aesthetic autonomy) has a general import and significance to the extent that it puts a clear question-mark against Deleuze and Guattari's more general reflections on the nature of the art-work in *What is Philosophy?* Third, and most significantly for us, posing the modernist problem in a Rancièrian or Badiouian manner has direct implications for the method of dramatization as we want to develop it. For, if the method of dramatization is, as we have argued, motivated by the prospect of bringing concepts to life and it turns out that Deleuze's and Deleuze and Guattari's concepts function merely to philosophically circumscribe in advance the aesthetic forms through which dramatization happens (cinema, language, architecture, painting and so on), then the method assumes a rather curious and abstract form. Although we will not be in a position to tease out the full implications of the second and third points in this chapter (a discussion that we will undertake in the next chapter), it is nonetheless necessary for us to be clear about the stakes involved in what might otherwise seem to be a treatment of the cinema books that is disconnected from the theme of dramatization.

So the focus in this chapter will be, in large part, on critically evaluating the modernist problem that is posed by Deleuze's work on cinema. That said, we will, towards the end of the chapter, put to work Deleuze's cinema books and Deleuze and Guattari's *Anti-Oedipus* in giving a brief reading of Paul Thomas Anderson's 1997 film *Boogie Nights*, a reading that will necessarily point us to chapter six and our encounter with Deleuze and Guattari's general aesthetics as they develop it in *What is Philosophy?*

The modernist problem

Jacques Rancière's *Film Fables* is the most obvious place to look when considering his critique of Deleuze's cinematic modernism (Rancière, 2006). The broad claim developed in *Film Fables* can be summed up thus: Deleuze's cinema books offer an aesthetically modernist meta-language and meta-narrative that is, at times, simply downloaded onto the narrative and plot of cinematic texts in a way that belies Deleuze's own taste for formalist or taxonomic analysis. Rancière asks us to consider, for example, Deleuze's discussion of Hitchcock's work at the end of *Cinema 1*. In this text, Deleuze presents Hitchcock's cinema as the throwing into crisis of the 'classical' cinema of the 'movement-image', a 'crisis' or 'rupture' that paves the way for the emergence of the 'modern' cinema of the 'time-image' (Deleuze, 1992, 205). Hitchcock's films loosen what Deleuze calls the 'sensory-motor link or schema'. That is to say, the links between action and reaction in plot or narrative, between situation and action, start to crack and we begin to glimpse the immersion or immobilization of characters in pure sound and optical situations. For example, 'the hero of *Rear Window*', says Deleuze, 'is reduced as it were to a pure optical situation' (Deleuze, 1992, 205). Rancière suggests that this rather formal and general analysis of the crisis and rupture of the movement-image and the emergence of a supposedly non-narrative modern time-image seems 'a bit strange' precisely because it is developed by drawing on aspects of plot or features of the narrative situation. 'It is hard to see', Rancière suggests, 'in what ways the characters' motor or psychomotor problems hinder the linear arrangement of the images' (Rancière, 2006, 115). For instance, when we recall the opening shots in *Rear Window* of L.B. Jeffries' apartment (shots which reveal the immobilized photo-journalist), the shots come to us in a linear and narrative fashion. The formal apparatus or structure of Hitchcock's cinema (the sequencing of shots) is not, Rancière points out, immobilized by Jeffries' broken leg. Or, to take another example, 'Hitchcock's camera is not paralysed by Scottie's vertigo' (Rancière, 2006, 115). So, if the logic or apparatus of the movement-image is not at all immobilized or paralysed by the fictional characters or narrative situation, how then can Deleuze draw on characters and situations in narrative or classical cinema to argue for the emergence of the modern time-image? Rancière gives what we might consider a rather caustic response to this question:

> The only…alternative is to consider the paralysis symbolic, to say that Deleuze treats fictional situations of paralysis as simple allegories emblematic of the rupture in the…sensory-motor link. However, if Deleuze has to allegorise this rupture by means of emblems taken from stories, isn't it because it cannot be identified as an actual difference between types of images? Isn't it because the theoretician of the cinema must find a visible incarnation for a purely ideal rupture? The movement-image is "in crisis" because the thinker needs it to be. (Rancière, 2006, 116)

Rancière suggests that the reason Deleuze needs the movement-image to be in crisis is because he is committed to a modernist idea that it is revolutions or ruptures in the arts that developmentally manifest their proper essence or autonomy. 'The novelty of the "modern" is', says Rancière, 'that the essence of the art, though it had always been active in the art's previous manifestations, has now gained its autonomy' (Rancière, 2006, 108). Indeed, in Deleuze's dramatization of the crisis in the classical cinema of the movement-image and the emergence of the modern cinema of the time-image (where, for example, the loosening of the sensory-motor-link in Hitchcock is more fully and autonomously developed in the modern cinema of the French new wave or

Italian neo-realism), Rancière finds a clearly modernist and redemptive discourse in which the 'crisis' or the 'rupture' is but an 'episode in the edifying narrative through which each art proves it own artistry'. In this way, 'Deleuze's division between a movement-image and a time-image doesn't escape...modernist theory' (Rancière, 2006, 108).

Although quite particular and pointed, Rancière's critique of Deleuze in this context can be thought to have a more general import and significance. From the point of view of Deleuze and Guattari's method of dramatization, Rancière raises a troubling problem concerning how we are to approach cultural-aesthetic forms generally (cinema), and artworks in particular (a film like *Vertigo* or *Rear Window*). As we saw in chapter four, Deleuze and Guattari are keen to emphasize how a particular cultural form like language needs to be understood in a thoroughly pragmatic and concrete way, in accordance with its immanent capacity for intervening in, and dramatizing, the world through, say, 'humour', through 'slogans', 'incorporeal transformations' and so on. But, this investment in the idea that a cultural or aesthetic form like language performs dramatic functions of various sorts may indeed presuppose a meta-language (pragmatics) and a meta-narrative (the sub-discipline of pragmatics emerges from the 'rubbish dumps' of linguistics to become fundamental not only to the study of language-use in speech action, but crucial to a critique of the other branches of linguistic science such as syntactics, semantics and so on) that remains in a rather curious and abstract relation to the moments and experiences of dramatization as such. Indeed, the questions that we raised against Deleuze and Guattari's modernist pragmatics in our concluding remarks of chapter four resonate, in a general way, with Rancière's critique of Deleuze's cinema books. In both cases we are left wondering whether a philosophical meta-narrative and meta-language helps or hinders when it comes to understanding what materially happens when we experience how a cultural form or an art-work performs its dramatizing function.

Coming back specifically to Deleuze's writings on cinema, we can see that this general concern about philosophical or meta-linguistic abstraction even crops up in the work of scholars who are very sympathetic to this body of work. For instance, both David Rodowick and Ian Buchanan raise the spectre of 'the popular' against Deleuze. In *Gilles Deleuze's Time Machine*, Rodowick admits that he find some aspects of the Deleuze's cinema books indefensible. Deleuze's auteurism and Parisian cinephilism seem to feed into a cultural elitism that renders the cinema books something of an 'anachronism', by which Rodowick means that Deleuze remains committed to an Adorno-style modernism that is somewhat exhausted (Rodowick, 1997, 211). Writing in the mid 1990s, Rodowick argues: 'In an era when postmodernism's critique of hierarchies of value predominates, Deleuze's theory of modernism often evokes a perspective where the last avatars of experimentation and thought in film are defending cinematic art from the onslaught of a one-dimensional mass culture' (Rodowick, 1997, xiv). In a much more recent collection, *Deleuze and the Schizoanalysis of Cinema*, Ian Buchanan, like Rodowick, clearly sees the connections between Deleuze's cinematic modernism and the modernist aesthetics of Adorno and the Frankfurt School (Buchanan, 2008, 6–7). And like Rodowick, Buchanan's reading of Deleuze is very much located 'after' the provocation of postmodernism, or at least postmodernism in the form famously presented to us by Jameson (1991). Consider the following passage where Buchanan speaks to Deleuze's modernist intuition that we should look to what is exceptional, innovative, thought-provoking, new, singular, or interesting rather than the judging or worrying about the seemingly endless circulation of dross in cinematic production. Buchanan writes:

> Deleuze would probably have no qualms about rejecting the bulk of contemporary cinema as cretinizing schlock...but would no doubt add that such judgements are of little use.... So rather than moralize about the vacuity of Hollywood, I expect Deleuze would instead have us continue to sift the dross in search for that rare nugget of innovation. In this sense, Jameson is surely correct to describe Deleuze as a modernist, but it is precisely for this reason that we need to *reverse* Deleuze and look not at the exceptions to the rule of a generalized nullity in cinema he identifies, but at the nullity itself – sexploitation films, blaxploitation films, direct to video shockers, sequels.... Nowhere does Deleuze write about *Hell Behind Bars, Shaft, Night of the Living Dead, The Birds 2* or even *Star Wars* (which when he wrote his cinema books was the highest grossing film of all time), yet this is the *real* Hollywood. (Buchanan, 2008, 10–11)

If Buchanan insists on this *reversal* of Deleuze's cinematic modernism then this is clearly because he believes, with Jameson, that popular films – that is, the 'sexploitation films, blaxploitation films, direct to video shockers, sequels and prequels, remakes and rip-offs, blockbusters and stinkers' – need to be critically engaged with as they are, as he says, 'the bread and butter of Hollywood, the stuff on which the industry sustains itself' (Buchanan, 2008, 11). The modernist insistence on a cinematic exceptionalism, the implicit injunction to 'sift through the dross in search for that rare nugget of innovation', trades on an aesthetic and moral-political binary (good/bad, innovative/clichéd, shocking/tired...) that places the vast majority of films beyond Deleuze's concern, and this, for Buchanan, is clearly a problem. If, for example, Hollywood is a dominant player in the production and circulation of cinematic images, then should we not bring whatever conceptual tools we have to bear on it? This is obviously Buchanan's point, and he suggests that those conceptual tools can be found by turning to Deleuze and Guattari's later collaborative works, particularly *Anti-Oedipus*. Buchanan's move here, to work against the worst excesses or more problematic aspects of Deleuze's modernism by supplementing it with Deleuze and Guattari's collaborative work, is an interesting and useful one. Indeed, later in the chapter, we will consider Deleuze's comments in *Cinema 2* concerning the connection (the 'conspiracy' as he rather dramatically puts it) between cinematic production and money, using Deleuze and Guattari's *Anti-Oedipus* to help us think through how this connection is made or cinematically dramatized in Paul Thomas Anderson's 1997 film *Boogie Nights*. For the moment, though, let us shift focus somewhat in order to directly pose a question that is important to any discussion of cinematic modernism: namely, does cinema have the capacity or autonomy to think or engender thought?

Can cinema think?

The question of whether cinema (or indeed any art-form) can think may be usefully posed in terms of a problem concerning its medium-specificity or singular uniqueness. This, in a sense, is the point that Rancière makes when he suggests a redemptive narrative in modernism – namely that the crisis and ruptures can be followed in such a way as to track the increasing purification of the particular form, the emergence of its singular uniqueness. That is to say, an art-form 'proves it own artistry' to the extent that it has gained an 'autonomy' that was not possible in 'the art's previous manifestations'. We might be tempted to think that Rancière's remarks here, directed as they are at Deleuze's cinema books, miss their mark in bringing to mind more the kind of naïve progressivism found in, say, the art-criticism of Clement Greenberg. Greenberg's (1992) famous thesis on 'modernist painting', we recall, essays how the autonomy of the modernist painting is developed to the extent that the form becomes purified in medium-specific terms. Painting becomes entrenched, as Greenberg argues, more firmly in its own area of competence and no longer remains parasitic on, or derivative of, other forms such as theatre or sculpture. Put simply, Greenberg argues that painting as a form can think purely in painterly terms; that is, in accordance with a 'flat surface', 'properties of pigment', the 'enclosing shape of the frame' and so on (Greenberg, 1992).

It is interesting to note that Deleuze seems to make some Greenberg-esque noises in the cinema books. For instance, at the beginning the seventh chapter of *Cinema 2*, Deleuze speaks of the promise of cinema as an 'industrial art' capable of 'automatic movement', a movement that aims to work on thought, providing a shock to thought (a 'nooshock' as he calls it) that, in turn, forces thinking anew. Or as Deleuze explicitly puts it in the opening lines of the chapter:

> Those who first made and thought about cinema began from a sim-ple idea: cinema as industrial art achieves self-movement, automatic movement, it makes movement the immediate given of the image. This kind of movement no longer depends on a moving body or an object which realizes it.... It is the image which itself moves in itself.... It could be said that this was already the case with all artis-tic images; and Eisenstein constantly analyzes the paintings of Da Vinci and El Greco as if they were cinematographic images.... But pictorial images are nevertheless immobile in themselves so it is the mind which has to "make" movement.... It is only when movement becomes automatic that the artistic essence of the image is realized; producing a shock to thought, communicating vibrations to the cor-tex, touching the nervous and cerebral system directly. (Deleuze, 1989, 156)

There is plenty of evidence from the above passage to justify Rancière's suggestion that Deleuze is, at least partly, motivated by a Greenberg-esque progressivism. Although, rather than talking specifically about the progressive purification of a particular form (however, Rancière would claim that this is implicit in the supposed transition from the movement-image to the time-image), we see Deleuze here presenting a narrative in which cinema emerges to offer the promise of an 'image which itself moves in itself'. Importantly, though, this promise (latent in the painterly images of Da Vinci or El Greco, but remaining essentially 'immobile' or in an abstract relation to the 'mind' which has to 'make movement' out of these images) can only be made good with a cin-ema in which 'movement becomes automatic' and it is here the 'artistic essence of the image is realized'. The significance of this, of course, is that automatic movement in the image works on thought, shocks thought, disrupts thought, and potentially engenders new thought. How? What are we to take from Deleuze's suggestion that images can communicate 'vibrations to the cortex, touching the nervous and cerebral system directly'? Again, we need to consider this in terms of medium specificity: as the promise of what a new, or emerging, technological apparatus or form is capable of producing, and producing in thought. In a sense, it would be quite easy here to montage or cross-cut from Deleuze to the 'medium theory' of, say, Marshall McLuhan and the suggestion that 'man', 'consciousness', 'thought' is extended and reshaped across space and time by media such as cinema (McLuhan, 1964). Cinema touches the cortex, or connects to the brain directly, precisely because it is operationalized as (or simply is) a technics of sensation, perception and so on. As a technological apparatus, a technics of sensation and perception, cinema thinks, and thinks in its own cinematic terms. As spectators of cinema (or visual images/culture more generally) we think in relation to this new form of thinking, rethinking our relation to technological and aesthetic forms as a consequence. The result being we think differently or 're-mediate' (we, say, read Jane Austen's novels cinematically, or Dickens televisually and so on). Although she does not mention medium theory specifically, Claire Colebrook (2006) emphasizes the importance of the cinema as technological apparatus that thinks and provokes thinking in this way. She writes:

> [C]inema is a technology that allows us – humans possessed of a brain that bears an entire history of thought – to rethink our relation to technology, recognizing that our history is itself technological, a history made up of reconfiguring, mutating and proliferating machines. Cinema is the encounter between the machine of the brain-eye-body and the machine of the camera-screen. And it is this encounter that opens thought to the history of the human, and, if pushed further, allows thought to transcend the human. The cinematic technology that apparently supplements and constitutes the human opens onto the inhuman. (Colebrook, 2006, 10)

Of course, while it is all very well to formally suggest that cinema (as technological apparatus) autonomously thinks in its own cinematic terms and that, consequently, it provokes new thinking, there still remains a political question concerning film content and our everyday experiences of what is thought in and through the images we are constantly confronted with. This, again, would be one of the implications that follow from a Rancièrian critique of the cinema books. Put simply, is there a sense in which a cinema of the 'nooshock' remains too formal and technical, that it exhibits no real desire to engage with the more banal and everyday experience of encountering cinematic or other images? It is worth noting that in provocative and dramatic works (Rancière is every bit the dramatist Deleuze and Guattari are) such as *The Ignorant Schoolmaster, The Philosopher and his Poor* and *The Nights of Labour*, Rancière never tires of cautioning against the danger of intellectuals thumbing their noses at those dreary and banal subjects or classes who supposedly lack what they themselves possess: namely, the aesthetic and political self-reflexivity needed to institute social and political change for the better (Rancière, 1989; 1991; 2003). Rancière's critical point is that such intellectualism never develops or fosters a taste for these supposedly banal or dreary subjects and classes and, if it did, it may well be surprised by the complicated picture that would emerge (Davis, 2010). So, to put the question pointedly, is Deleuze, as a philosopher engaging with cinema, implicated here? Does his thinking on cinematic thinking lack some important complication?

We might want to concede that it is indeed rather limited to speak of cinema as a technological apparatus that opens the human onto the inhuman, thought to non-thought, to its outside. And we also think it is always important to bear in mind that, techno-hoopla aside, the political significance of cinema as a technological apparatus needs to be interrogated in terms of the ways it rationalizes, legitimizes or natural-izes ways of seeing, knowing, feeling, being. This is not to suggest that scholarly work that has tried to come to grips with the provocation of Deleuze's thinking about the cine-technology is unimportant or trivial, but that it has sometimes lacked a desire for the banal and dreary, where the 'banal' and 'dreary' gestures precisely towards the social and politi-cal consequences that attend to the way the cinematic apparatus func-tions to reproduce ways of seeing, knowing, feeling, being (we might think of this as the more banal ideological work performed by a cinema of mass consumption). This accusation, implicit in Rancière and indeed explicit in Buchanan, would indeed seem to apply to Deleuze. That said, and as Buchanan is aware, it is a critique of Deleuze that is already pitching at a moving target. That is to say, the Deleuze of the cinema books is already concerned with the ideological work performed by a cinema of mass consumption. Indeed, if we come back to the begin-ning of the seventh chapter of *Cinema 2* we can see immediately that Deleuze raises the idea of cinema as 'nooshock' with some important complication: that is, as a 'claim'. Yes, cinema claims for itself the possi-bility that it may be a 'shock to thought', that it may provoke a thought capable of changing the world, but is there any evidence to suggest that cinema can actually do this? Writing from the vantage point of the late-twentieth-century, Deleuze, while undoubtedly still moved by this notion, acknowledges its pretension. As he says: the idea of a political cinema capable of imposing a shock to the thought of the masses 'raises a smile today' (Deleuze, 1989, 157).

Notwithstanding Rancière's perceptive and provocative critique of the cinema books, we think it would be unduly harsh and simplistic to say that Deleuze exhibits an intellectualism that is haughty and indifferent to the social and political consequences that follow from the way the cinematic apparatus functions to reproduce certain ways of seeing, feeling, being, and so on. We agree with Buchanan that Deleuze exhibits exceptionalist tendencies in his cinema work. He constructs a 'modernist canon', as Lecercle also points out in the context of his literary modernism, believing that 'there are great texts' and 'that the task of the philosopher-critic is to define them and extol their greatness' (Lecercle, 2010, 119). But such exceptionalism, such a desire for a 'modernist canon' (Vertov, Hitchcock, Godard and so on), springs from a particular kind of political dissatisfaction and a critical sense of how, more broadly speaking, cinema as a mass industrial art-form dramatizes and brings to life concepts that work only to sustain us in our acquiescence to what we might otherwise consider intolerable social and political situations. Although it is not unproblematic to say so (as it goes explicitly against Deleuze and Guattari's constant emphasis on the importance of affirmation and joy), there is real moral-political anger, frustration, maybe even some melancholy, sparking off those pages in the cinema books where Deleuze talks about how a contemporary experience of the cinema of mass consumption is one drowning in cliché and dripping in money. And when Deleuze says that the notion of a political cinema that can change the world and engage the masses 'raises a smile today', it is hard not to feel that the smile is, in part, a rather melancholic one, or at the very least a smile through gritted teeth, a knowing smile that bears witness to the clichéd and repetitive manner in which cinema as an industrial art performs its magic in the service of the commodity-form. 'Cinema is dying', says Deleuze rather dramatically, 'from its quantitative mediocrity' (Deleuze, 1989, 164).

Cliché and Money

Let us be clear and rather declarative on this point: the Deleuze of the cinema books wants to insist on the idea that the contemporary experience of the cinema of mass consumption is one drowning in cliché and dripping in money, and that this is of the utmost political-economic significance (Deleuze, 1992, xiv). Let us take the notion of cliché first. Cliché is a key concept for Deleuze, and for Deleuze and Guattari's cultural and political theory (Porter, 2009; 2010). We already have a sense of the importance of the cliché from our discussion of Deleuze and Guattari's pragmatics in the previous chapter. Recall the notion of the cliché as an easy-to-hand reserve of ready-made expressions and thoughts that allow us to regulate, pattern and order the world and our social interactions within it. What we now need to add to this is the important connection that the cliché has to what Deleuze and Guattari would call the 'intolerable'. In *Anti-Oedipus*, Deleuze and Guattari, drawing explicitly on Spinoza, pose for them what is a key question concerning the 'intolerable', the key question of political philosophy as they see it: 'Why do men fight for their servitude as stubbornly as though it were their salvation?" How can people possibly reach the point of shouting: "More taxes! Less bread!?'" (Deleuze and Guattari, 1984, 29). In other words, how is it that we can put up with situations that are intolerable? How is it that we come to desire our own servitude, our own suppression? Deleuze's answer to this question in the cinema books is pointed: the intolerable becomes tolerable in and through the 'sensory-motor evasions' that are mediated by the cliché. That is to say, it is the cliché that allows us to tolerate the intolerable because it allows us to evade or take flight from it. Consider the following, strikingly powerful, passage from the first chapter of *Cinema 2*:

We see, and we more or less experience, a powerful organization of poverty and oppression. And we are precisely not without sensory-motor schemata for recognizing such things, for putting up and approving of them and for behaving ourselves subsequently, taking into account our situation, our capabilities and our tastes. We have schemata for turning away when it is too unpleasant, for prompting resignation when it is terrible…. It should be pointed out here that even metaphors are sensory-motor evasions, and furnish us with something to say when we no longer know what to do: they are specific schemata of an affective nature. Now this is what a cliché is. A cliché is a sensory-motor image of the thing. As Bergson says, we do not perceive the thing or the image in its entirety, we always perceive less of it, we perceive only what we are interested in perceiving, or rather what it is in our interest to perceive, by virtue of our economic

interests, ideological beliefs and psychological demands. We therefore normally perceive clichés. (Deleuze, 1989, 20)

For us, this passage will be worth considering against the backcloth of the
persisting *modernist problem* that is at play in Deleuze's cinema work. But
before we do so, some clarity is needed again about the stakes involved
in posing this problem. As we have seen, the modernist problem in
Deleuze (and Guattari's) work concerns (among other things) a charge
of philosophical and meta-linguistic abstraction and, with Rancière, the
rather caustic suggestion that the modernist thinker miraculously finds
in the given art-work or art-form concepts uncannily similar to their
own. In other words, the philosopher approaches the art-work with a
desire to invest it with the autonomy to think, but, in truth, all the
thinking has been done by the philosopher in advance. So when, for
example, Deleuze talks in the cinema books about comparing the great
directors in the history of cinema 'not only with painters, architects and
musicians, but also with thinkers', investing in the idea that they 'think
with movement-images and time-images instead of concepts', Deleuze,
for Rancière, is making a classic modernist move of trying to gloss a
rather paternalist-philosophical pedagogy with the ideological veneer
of aesthetic autonomy. That is to say, the philosopher claims no hierarchy exists between his disciplinary practice and aesthetic practices, suggesting that the form of thinking subsequently attributed to the latter is
its autonomous preserve or property. This could explain Deleuze's suggestion that the cinema books offer a 'taxonomy', or 'natural history' of
cinema, 'an attempt at the classification of images and signs' (Deleuze,
1992, xiii). He is not doing a 'history of cinema' that over-contextualizes
the medium in advance, but is merely attributing concepts to a mode
of thinking (image-thinking) always-already at work in the art-form as
such; a philosophy that resonates or works alongside cinema, but which
claims no priority over it. As Deleuze, rather modestly, puts it in his
concluding reflections of *Cinema 2*: 'A theory of cinema is not "about"
cinema, but about the concepts that cinema gives rise to' and 'the practice of concepts', or philosophy as film theory, can have 'no privilege
over' other practices (Deleuze, 1989, 280).

Of course, the caustic, Rancièrian, response at this point would be
to say that Deleuze is being too modest, falsely modest even, to the
extent that his key concepts (movement-image and time-image) still
imply a pedagogy whereby the modernist thinker teaches us not what
cinema thinks on its own (Rancière refers to this paradoxically as 'a
thought that does not think' precisely because it is said to be immanent

to the form or work), but rather how we *ought* to think about cinema, and think about it in abstraction. Badiou would wholeheartedly concur with this. Indeed, in *Deleuze*, Badiou suggests that Deleuze's cinema books, pressed very hard as they are into the service of his philosophy, will actually leave genuine lovers of the cinema rather cold and indifferent (Badiou, 2000, 15). The cinema books, despite their many case studies of directors and schools of filmmaking, and despite many 'supple individual film descriptions', are dominated by Deleuze's abstract and impersonal concepts of 'movement and time'. Like Rancière, Badiou is decidedly caustic in his remarks about the philosophical and pedagogical reductionism of Deleuze's work on cinema. He writes:

> One the one hand, Deleuze singularly analyzes work after work, with the disconcerting erudition of the non-specialist. Yet, on the other hand, what finally comes out of this is siphoned into the reservoir of concepts that, from the very beginning of the work, Deleuze has established and linked together: namely movement and time.... This is why film buffs have always found it difficult to make use of the two hefty volumes of the cinema. (Badiou, 2000, 15)

And again:

> When all is said and done, the multiple rippling of cases that are evoked by Deleuze's prose have only an adventitious value. What counts is the impersonal power of the concepts themselves.... Ultimately, concepts... are only attached to the initial concrete case in their movement and not in what they give to thought. This is why, in the volumes on cinema, what one learns concerns the Deleuzean theory of movement and time, and the cinema gradually becomes neutralized and forgotten. (Badiou, 2000, 16)

Let us begin to come back, then, to Deleuze's remarks on cliché in *Cinema 2* in light of these Badiouian and Rancièrian critiques. From a Deleuzean perspective, there is a sense in which both Badiou and Rancière trade on the worst, most reductive, clichés when they critically evaluate Deleuze's cinema books. Deleuze becomes a rather unforgiving didactic figure, tying cinema (and the art-work more generally) to his Bergsonian philosophy of 'movement and time'. From this point of view, philosophy performs, what Badiou in his *Handbook of Inaesthetics* would call, 'the educational surveillance of art's purpose' (Badiou, 2005b, 5). Sociologically or institutionally speaking (and we speak as institutionalized English-speaking academics), there is no doubting the pertinence and critical purchase of Badiou's phrasing here as it clearly chimes with an experience of the increasing influence that the Deleuzean meta-language of 'movement and time' now exerts over screen studies in the Anglophone world and its corresponding academic marketplace. That Deleuze should become a cliché not only to his critics, but also a marketable cliché at the hands of those who supposedly seek to extol his greatness, is hardly surprising (the potential fate of all great thinkers no doubt). However that may be, the claim we want to develop is that a more genuinely sympathetic understanding and engagement with what Deleuze suggests by way of the notion of the 'cliché' can be more productive than caustic baiting, or (dare we say it, yes let's say it in earnest and without even the slightest whiff of irony) reducing his thinking to a brand aimed at target markets.

Clichés, as Deleuze says in the passage in question, 'furnish us with something to say when we no longer know what to do'. We would suggest that while Badiou and Rancière have a lot to say about Deleuze, the philosopher, they exhibit no genuine feeling that it might be productive to view him (and Guattari) as dramatists or, in the terms of our preferred reading here, as practitioners of a method of dramatization. Why not read Deleuze's words for their dramatic effects? Perhaps the critical and caustic gesture of continually fixating on the philosopher's meta-language or concepts (the obsession of the philosopher's mastery over the art-work) simply misses the point of their already writerly, and aesthetically self-reflexive, form – concepts which have already assumed the modality of dramatic effects. As we emphasized in chapter four, Deleuze and Guattari's writing (say, their use of slogans) is performatively and consciously writerly in form: they practice 'philosophy as a kind of writing, with a venegance' (Lecercle, 2010, 128). Also, in the last chapter, we suggested, with Williams, that Deleuze (and Guattari's) claims can, and should, be read as 'smiling provocations', although the claims concerning the cliché in *Cinema 2* are better read in connection to a smile which quickly becomes a grimace, a smile through gritted teeth, as we put it earlier. Read in this way, Deleuze's words on the cliché assume a different emotional charge and can precipitate any number of hooks, provocations, connections, or complications (Williams, 2008, 20).

For instance, Deleuze's Bergsonian suggestion that cliché becomes part of our sensory-motor schema, a 'specific schemata of an affective nature', moves us to immediately complicate the concept. For the idea of the cliché as, say, ideological re-presentation (for example, the clichéd reproduction of identifiable generic conventions of a cinema of mass consumption; the repeatable, standardized and seeming infinitely exchangeable formulae of industrial production) only begins to make sense when we see it as immanent to a developing consciousness (that is, a desire for the generic convention and so on). Of course, Deleuze would want to insist that the clichés of industrial cinematic production reproduce, ideologically speaking, their own conditions (the commodity-form as repeatable, standardized and infinitely exchangeable) and that this is precisely intolerable because it becomes the seemingly 'permanent state of a daily banality' (Deleuze, 1989, 170). However, and to repeat the important point: the ideological work performed by a cinema of mass consumption becomes possible (the intolerable becomes tolerable, so to speak) only when the cliché becomes part of our developing consciousness and feel for things, part of our technics of sensation, perception and so on. 'Nothing but clichés, clichés everywhere…. Physical, optical, auditory clichés and psychic clichés mutually feed on each other. In order for people to be able to bear themselves and the world, misery has to reach inside consciousness and the inside has to be like the outside' (Deleuze, 1992, 208–9).

Deleuze's notion of cliché as a 'specific schemata of an affective nature' can have the dramatic effect of throwing us back onto our own cognitive resources, making us think about our own technics of sensation and perception, our own feel and consciousness of things, how that consciousness or feeling 'inside' relates to industrial cinematic production 'outside', and how that consciousness or feeling gives rise to the clichés that allow us to displace or bear the intolerable situation in which we find ourselves as spectators of cinema: say, our daily, weekly, monthly, desire for the banalities of a cinema of mass consumption that continually performs its magic in the service of the commodity-form. And rather than feeling that our Deleuze-inspired remarks on the cliché are overly dramatic or philosophically and pedagogically reductive (where the cinema of mass consumption is over-generalized, over-dramatized and consequently read in the abstract as the clichéd reproduction of the commodity-form), we can follow Deleuze's own example and begin to think of particular cinematic texts in and through which the cliché dramatically operates.

We can consider, by way of a brief example, Paul Thomas Anderson's 1997 film *Boogie Nights*. This Hollywood production is of interest from a Deleuzean perspective because of the particular way it thinks about the connections between the cliché and the commodity-form, or, more particularly, the relation between cliché, cinematic production and money. The drama that unfolds in *Boogie Nights* is one that provokes and moves us to think, as Deleuze would say, about money as a 'conspiracy' that is 'internal' or immanent to film as 'industrial art' (Deleuze, 1989, 77). Focusing on the function of money in the US porn industry in late 1970s and early 1980s, *Boogie Nights* dramatizes the cliché in a specific way: namely, as a productive response to the problem that money poses to cinematic production. We see this very clearly in the scene where the main character, Dirk Diggler, is first tasked to perform for the camera, his first sex scene. The cinematic apparatus and money form an important conjunction here and this gets dramatized by the way the camera moves away from Diggler and his female co-star and doubles back to the crew and director and then, most significantly, to the camera itself, showing us its inner movements or workings, showing us that the film stock is a finite resource, running out. Now, this image of the film stock running out is particularly suggestive from a Deleuzean (and Deleuze-Guattarian) perspective. Immediately, it explains or foregrounds the interruption in the flow of the scene being shot (that is, the actors are told to stop performing while the crew 'change mags'). Now, this can be read as a comment on the fact that porn does not, as Buchanan says in his interesting Deleuze–Guattarian reading of Larry Clarke's laudable documentary on the porn industry *Impaled*, 'show it all', but only 'displays that which can be coded as belonging to the domain of the sexual' (Buchanan, 2008, 44). That is to say, pornographic cinema as a capitalist enterprise or money machine effects, what the Deleuze and Guattari of *Anti-Oedipus* would call, 'relative breaks' in its flow in order to codify the sexual as a consumable product or commodity-form for a targeted market. Indeed, and to generalize somewhat, the notion of flows being effected by 'relative breaks', 'break-flow' as Deleuze and Guattari term it, importantly defines how contemporary 'capitalism' operates (Deleuze and Guattari, 1984, 246–7).

Let us come back specifically to the text of *Boogie Nights* to get a more concrete sense of this. Before the shooting of his first sex scene, Diggler is told in no uncertain terms that if he drops or fluffs a line that he should continue on regardless ('do not stop' is the repeated imperative from the crew). And we can, of course, understand this imperative as part of a response to the problem of money. For, as we know, the porn industry in the mid-to-late 1970s is still working with film rather than video, and this is a more expensive proposition in terms of production (a point dramatically underlined in the second half of *Boogie Nights* as it charts the move into video at the end of the 1970s and early 1980s). Now, we can think of the cliché of the fluffed line, and the cliché of disjointed and clunky dialogue, so characteristic of this genre in the era before video (and so skilfully captured by Thomas Anderson in the scene in question), as a productive response to the problem of money. And this is precisely what we mean when we suggested that *Boogie Nights* dramatizes the cliché (the fluffed line, the disjointed and clunky dialogue) as a productive response to the problem that money, as a finite resource, poses. There is a particular sense of 'break-flow' that is expressed in and through *Boogie Nights*. The action and narrative flows, to be sure, but the packaging of the sexual as a commodity-form or consumable object for a targeted audience can only be effected by the continual breaks (whether 'changing mags', lighting, camera position and so on) that are internal or immanent to its codification as such. *Boogie Nights* shows this 'break-flow' by focusing on the apparatus of cinematic production, by presenting the genre-specific cliché of the fluffed line and clunky dialogue which insists on continuing with the promise of narrative flow ('do not stop'), no matter how many lines get fluffed, no matter how badly the dialogue, the narrative, and ultimately the fantasy of an unmediated 'showing it all', gets broken up.

We have yet to mention perhaps the most obvious cliché of pornographic cinema. We are thinking, of course, about *the money shot* itself. This is a particular problem for *Boogie Nights*, as this rather mainstream Hollywood film on the porn industry does not, cannot, show us the money shot. Unsurprisingly, the problem is reproduced or doubled in the scene in question, as Diggler reaches orgasm without the interruption or break necessary to capture the money shot on film and in accordance with the required generic convention or formula. We have full sex, but minus the money shot, we 'see it all', but not quite according to the formula: no successful 'break-flow'. This, as we see, is a source of real concern for the director and the crew, a concern that is only alleviated when Diggler rather matter-of-factly informs them he can 'do it again, if they need a close-up'. It is at this point that the scene effectively ends, and we cut to a champagne cork being popped against the backcloth of celebratory music. Now, clearly, the popping champagne cork can be considered a symbolic or metaphorical money shot (no doubt precipitating a knowing smile among those spectators who get the joke), but perhaps what is more telling or significant about this is simply the fact that it is a flow codified in a particular way; that it circulates in order to be consumed by a targeted audience (a mainstream Hollywood audience). From the point of the Deleuze–Guattarian 'break-flow', there is no formal or substantive difference between the clichéd money shot in porn (flow of sperm) which supposedly 'shows it all', and its symbolic or metaphorical reproduction in a Hollywood production like *Boogie Nights* (flow of champagne). Both trade in the cliché of the money shot; both codify for an assumed and targeted market.

Cinema: the Philosopher's Plaything?

Perhaps this brief discussion of *Boogie Nights* does little more than confirm the fears of those critics like Rancière and Badiou who question the usefulness of Deleuze's work on cinema. Does the actual cinematic text of *Boogie Nights* simply give way to a discussion of Deleuze's concepts (the 'cliché', 'money')? Are we moved only to download Deleuze–Guattarian concepts (i.e., 'break-flow') and discuss such concepts in a way that 'neutralizes', as Badiou would say, the concreteness of the text? Do we learn nothing from *Boogie Nights*, save the Deleuzean and Deleuze–Guattarian concepts that we already knew in advance of our reading of the text? Does cinema become the philosopher's plaything or toy? Or, to generalize even further: have we simply been seduced by the philosopher's desire for mastery over the art-work?

Posing the question in this way helps to again bring into focus the more general import and significance the critical literature on Deleuze's cinema books has for his and Guattari's broader aesthetic concerns. And, of course, our concern here is to consider the implications that this critique may have for the method of dramatization. We have suggested that Rancière and Badiou insist on making the critical-caustic gesture of continually fixating on Deleuze's philosophically modernist meta-language and concepts, rather than seeing him, as Lecercle would say, as a literary modernist, a dramatist whose concepts have already assumed an aesthetically reflexive and writerly form (say, the slogan or the smiling provocation that moves us). To repeat our earlier rhetorical question: why not read Deleuze's words on cinema for their dramatic effects? Clearly, this could be seen as a rather strange and regressive move, particularly if it is viewed as an argument that tries to ground Deleuze's claims about the autonomy of cinema as a particular form (a form of thinking in images) with recourse to another form that is foreign to it and which compromises its medium-specificity (the provocation of thinking expressed in the use of words undoubtedly gives us images, but this not the same as the cinematic apparatus). But, what if we begun to view these forms (the images of cinema and the words of language) not only in their medium-specificity, but also by way of a more general function and connection? What then?

What if we insist that Deleuze's words in *Cinema 2* on the cliché and money have a dramatic effect of throwing us back onto our own cognitive resources, making us think about a familiar cinematic text like *Boogie Nights* in a new, or more unfamiliar, way? We are moved by words to think about cliché and money and we think about them in relation to a cinematic text that then thinks them cinematically. And if we characterize this cinematic thinking with certain words, this does not necessarily mean we rob it of autonomy, but rather we move toward a more complicated picture of connectedness between forms. For example, Deleuze and Guattari's words about the 'break-flow' in contemporary capitalism do, as Rancière would say, get illustrated in the narrative situation of *Boogie Nights* (Diggler's first sex scene is stopped to 'change mags', it is a 'relative break' which illustrates how the sexual gets coded as commodity-form). However, the 'break-flow' also finds its formal cinematic expression in the way the problem of the money shot gets dealt with (the cut from the sex scene to the popping champagne cork). This metaphorical money shot only makes sense in accordance with the 'break-flow' in the cutting and montage of the images (Diggler saying he can 'do it again', then the cut and the juxtaposition with the popping champagne cork).

So we have a more complicated picture of connectedness between forms emerging out of our reading of *Boogie Nights*. We have words ('cliché', 'money', 'break-flow') and their provocation and dramatic effect in making us think in relation to the cinematic text (the dramatization of cliché as a response to the problem of money), which then connects to the formal, and medium-specific, apparatus of the images we find in the text (the 'break-flow' not only as illustration, but as montage/cutting). In order to search for a general function that we might attribute to the art-work in light of this picture of connectedness (and we find ourselves by necessity speaking in more general terms precisely because we are cutting across media or aesthetic forms), we need to move on from Deleuze's cinema books to a consideration of Deleuze and Guattari's broader reflections on the nature of art in their final collaborative work: *What is Philosophy?* In many important respects, the series of questions that we have posed here, against Deleuze's cinema books and, by implication, Deleuze and Guattari's aesthetics more generally, tend to revolve around another question: *what happens when we dramatize?* For the method of dramatization, as we said right at the beginning of the chapter, will remain rather curious and abstract for as long as it is philosophically circumscribed by ready-made concepts that are attributed to it in advance. If we are to sustain the claim that the method of dramatization brings concepts to life, then we need to consider what is happening in the moment of dramatization, what conditions the emergence of concepts as they are dramatized as such. In other words, we have to approach the problem of events or, more particularly, the problem of what we will call 'dramatic events'.

6
Events and the Method of Dramatization

We have been grappling with the problem of Deleuze and Guattari's modernism, a problem that arises in their work on language and linguistics (chapter four), and which is brought into ever sharper focus through the critical reception of Deleuze's cinema books, particularly, the provocative and important critiques that we found in Rancière and Badiou (chapter five). As we saw in the previous chapter, the problem of Deleuze and Guattari's modernism orbits, in many important respects, around an issue of aesthetic autonomy. Indeed, many of the questions we posed in chapter five sought to shed some light on this issue. Can cinema think? Does Deleuze philosophically circumscribe cinema by downloading a philosophical meta-language on it? Was our Deleuze and Deleuze–Guattarian inspired reading of *Boogie Nights* just another example of this desire for philosophical mastery? Does cinema (or the art-work more generally) inevitably become the philosopher's plaything, subject to the whim of the philosopher's concepts? Or, to generalize even further: is the very notion of a philosophy of art or aesthetics always-already problematic by virtue of the fact that it is an act of appropriation which sabotages any autonomy or intrinsic significance that we may want to attribute to the art-form or art-work?

While there are many possible roads these questions concerning aesthetic autonomy could take us down, it is our view that they fundamentally imply a discussion about the nature of *events*. That is to say, the problem of modernism (and the attending questions concerning aesthetic autonomy we have been posing) brings into sharp relief the need to think about the logic of events. Why? Well, to ask whether cinema as an art-form can think, or whether philosophy can have a productive relationship with art, or, more particularly, whether the art-work can be thought or experienced as intrinsically significant, is to ask *what happens in the art-work*. As we have emphasized throughout the book, aesthetic and cultural forms can dramatize political concepts; that this, importantly, is (or can be) part of *what happens* (for example, that Belfast happens to emerge as a 'post-conflict city' to the extent that it gets dramatized through a variety of cultural-aesthetic forms such as property and urban development, film, television, local journalism, architecture and so on). What we want to insist on in this final chapter is the inextricable link between aesthetic and cultural forms (or, more generally put, the art-work), the event and the method of dramatization. At this stage of proceedings, it may seem that insisting on the connection between the art-work, the event and the method of dramatization is hardly earth-shattering news. Is it not simply the case that we are claiming that the method of dramatization implies that we (to recall our slogan from chapter three) *make an event of thought* – that thought becomes a live event or happening, where becoming 'live' then implies a particular art-work, media or range of media in and through which its liveness dramatically unfolds and is experienced (for instance, those moments or scenes in *Boogie Nights* which cinematically think, say, the problem of money, the cliché, and so on)?

Well, in a sense, yes, we are making this claim! But it would be a rather dramatic understatement to say that this claim is not without complication. For what we are suggesting here (and what we have been implying all along) is the possibility of having some kind of direct experience that has a significance that is intrinsic to the moment of dramatization as it occurs (whether in the art-work or elsewhere). We will refer to this experience as a *dramatic event*. Why all the fuss in making this suggestion? For surely we already, experientially, have a sense of what a dramatic event is. Indeed, to the extent that we think about events, we tend to think of them as dramatic occurrences: the novel and unexpected things that happen to and around us. These can range from the small incidents that catch us unawares to being swept up in large-scale movements that challenge political regimes. It may be that they are intensely personal (the revelation of a loved-one), or profoundly collective (the formation of work-place solidarity amongst formerly alienated colleagues). They can occur in an instant or stretch over years. Whatever modalities an event assumes, we are aware that something dramatic is happening. We sense that this is not merely another occurrence among the many that make up our days; it is an event. In other words, we typically differentiate events from mere occurrences on the grounds that events contain within them something novel and unexpected, something dramatic; whatever that may be. And yet, dramatic events, and this explains the fuss we are making, remain problematic by nature, as the following comparison of Deleuze (and Guattari) with Badiou will reveal.

The problem with dramatic events

The respective philosophies of Deleuze (and Guattari) and Badiou represent two of the most significant and systematic attempts in contemporary thought to address directly the problematic nature of dramatic events. What is particularly significant for us is the way in which these philosophies of the event immediately put a clear question mark against our intuition that it is possible to directly experience a dramatic event, that there is an intrinsic significance to dramatic events *qua events*. We need, therefore, to delve into Deleuze's and Badiou's philosophies of events. This montage of Badiou's and Deleuze's concepts of the event will then allow us, towards the end of the chapter, to reassert, in a more refined form, our claim that it is possible to have a direct experience that has a significance intrinsic to the moment of dramatization as it occurs, that it is possible to experience a dramatic event from within its dramatic or aesthetic unfolding as such. Indeed, we shall conclude our discussions by working through the suggestion (one that draws strongly on elements of Deleuze and Guattari, and indeed Badiou, but also departs from them in important ways) that dramatic events can be productively described *as works of art*. But, before we get way ahead of ourselves, it is important to directly address the question of why, in the first instance, Deleuze and Badiou would be reluctant to agree to the suggestion that dramatic events can have intrinsic significance.

If, for example, we consider their responses to *les événements* of 'May '68' we can understand both Deleuze's and Badiou's reticence to accord dramatic events intrinsic significance. Against those on the left who mistakenly thought that May '68 was the beginning of a fully-fledged world-changing revolutionary moment and those, typically on the right, who treated it as a merely accidental collision of largely irrational forces, Deleuze and Badiou (eventually come to) agree that the 'eventness' of dramatic moments like May '68 can only be articulated by locating the drama outside the particular conjunctions of the moment itself. In the end, therefore, they agree that it is necessary to engage in, what Deleuze referred to as, 'a double battle' when thinking about the nature of the event: 'to thwart all dogmatic confusion between event and essence, and also every empiricist confusion between event and accident' (Deleuze, 1990, 4). On the one hand, there is the need to resist the tendency to treat events as the unfolding of some underlying historical process; on the other, the tendency to reduce events to the realm of the utterly contingent must be equally resisted. Whatever significance events have, and they agree that events are significant, we can only trace this significance if it is differentiated from experiences of actually occurring dramatic events, such as May '68. In other words, they both argue that the nature of an event *qua event* is not to be found by filling it up with essence or by emptying it of all significance but by looking for the drama outside of the dramatic moment itself.

Their desire to resist empiricist and dogmatist traps led them in different directions in their search for the significance of events. Deleuze argues for, what we will call, a *pre-occurrence* approach to significance, whereas Badiou argues that we must look to a *post-occurrence* account of their significance. As we saw in our discussions in the first part of the book (in chapter three particularly), Deleuze in several of his works, but especially *Difference and Repetition,* develops the idea that the real drama of the event is to be found in changes within the intensive (virtual) relationships that condition our extensive (actual) experience; therefore, *prior* to our experience of the dramatic event. Alternatively, in *Being and Event* and *Logics of Worlds*, it is clear that Badiou traces the significance of events into the future: he follows the trajectory of our experience through to the act of fidelity to the logical outcomes of certain situations *after* the dramatic event. The point here, for us, is that neither Deleuze nor Badiou locate the significance of events *within* our experience of actual dramatic occurrences for fear of falling prey to empiricism (events would then have no significance distinct from mere or utterly contingent occurrences) or dogmatism (events would then be endowed in advance with 'fate' or other essential qualities). For both thinkers, while they do require that the event retain an experiential dramatic dimension (Deleuze, of course, speaks of the two-fold nature of the event as virtual and actual; Badiou of the evental site that appears in the situation), the *significance* of the event is ultimately distanced from our experience of it, in order to express its dramatic quality.

This, as we have said, poses a real problem for the method of dramatization, at least as we want to develop it, precisely because it would seem to disallow the possibility of experiencing the significance of a dramatic event from within. Or, as we can now say, the problem here relates to an empiricism (the collapse of the event into utterly contingent occurrences, thus the loss of significance) or dogmatism (the circumscription of the of the event by way of an essentializing logic that captures and appropriates it in advance, thus the loss of its novelty) that would seem to plague us as we seek to accord the dramatic event intrinsic significance. It is worth spending a brief moment or two bringing into view how these general problems of empiricism and dogmatism have already made their presence felt (albeit implicitly) in the critical questions we have been posing in the previous couple of chapters.

For example, let us again consider the account of language developed in chapter four. Recall, towards the end of chapter, how we began to question this, raising the charge of linguistic and political idealism against a *modernist pragmatics* that insists, among other things, on incorporeal, virtual or evental sense. This charge of linguistic and political idealism connects to the problem of empiricism. The problem or concern being that we make the event of language (we mean this, of course, in the Deleuze'–Guattarian sense of 'incorporeal transformations', the capacity of language, mediated through the use of slogans say, to directly impact on social-political formations and change them) dependent on a pragmatics that reduces it to the utterly contingent (in this case the 'context' or 'circumstance' of its actualization). This concern is undoubtedly operating in the questions that concluded the chapter, namely: how does Deleuze and Guattari's modernist pragmatics differ from a more familiar pragmatics that would simply point to the particular context or circumstances of enunciation?; how can we insist, as Deleuze and Guattari do, on the capacity or autonomy of language to intervene and directly shape the social-political world, while, at the same time, seemingly explaining incorporeal transformations against the backcloth of collective assemblages?; are collective assemblages just another fancy name for what pragmatists call context or circumstances? Going back to the 'postulates of linguistics' plateau, we can see that this is clearly a worry for Deleuze and Guattari. To repeat the question that they pose in this context: 'when we use a word as vague as "intervene"... are we not still prey to a kind of idealism in which the slogan instantaneously falls from the sky?' (Deleuze and Guattari, 1988, 81). Or, to put the question more pointedly and positively from an empiricist-pragmatist perspective: rather than talking about the event of language, virtual sense and 'incorporeal transformations' etc., would we not be better off with an empiricism that looks to analyze the particular circumstances of language-use?

In many respects, Deleuze and Guattari's response is to doggedly insist that any form of empiricism brought to bear on language from some supposedly external point of view will fail to understand fully the medium it is working with. That is to say, we can talk empirically about the pragmatics of language, the various and varying 'contexts' or 'circumstances' in which it operates, but, for as long as we do so, we importantly miss out the event of language as such (again, or in this case, the potential it has for affecting the social-political body through 'incorporeal transformations'). As they put it: 'The general term "circumstances" should not leave the impression that it is a question of external circumstances. "I Swear" is not the same when said in the family, at school, in a love affair, in a secret society... [and] neither is it the same incorporeal transformation' (Deleuze, 1988, 82). In order to actually account for the dynamism or movement of language (its shifting affects on various bodies in different sets of circumstances) we need an immanent conception of how the medium of language works; we need to think about the event of language, virtual sense, 'incorporeal transformations' and so on.

Of course, the problem with certain forms of empiricism or 'linguistic science', from a Deleuze–Guattarian perspective, is that it presupposes an outside to language, a space or safe distance from which to understand and analyze language in accordance with 'linguistic constants' or, what they would also call, 'molar' concepts (the general notion of 'circumstances' or 'context' can be seen to perform this function in pragmatics). But to approach the outside of language or, what amounts to the same thing, account for its movement and dynamism, we need to see it as 'immanent to language' (Deleuze and Guattari, 1988, 82). This means that the very possibility of speaking in relatively settled dualist terms about language and its outside is inevitably complicated by the 'continual variations' that immanently express its movement as such: both 'language' and its 'outside' are, as Deleuze and Guattari say, 'inseparable from a movement of deterritorialization that carries them away' (Deleuze and Guattari, 1988, 87).

Coming back to the method of dramatization, we can see how the problem of empiricism in relation to events impacts on any attempt to put the method to work in language. It is a problem of the movement of language, its continual variation, and of empiricism becoming, paradoxically, an abstraction that fails to account for the real movement in the medium, of empiricism resting content with the false movement of uncomplicated dualism ('langue' and 'parole', 'competence' and 'performance' etc.).

Turning to the problem of dogmatism, it is clear that this can be related to Deleuze's cinematic modernism, that the Rancièrian and Badiouian objections raised against Deleuze's cinema books can be recast in light of this problem. The basic charge, to restage it in the terminology of this chapter, is this: Deleuze circumscribes the event of cinema by way of a philosophical logic that captures and appropriates it in advance, thus robbing it of its potential novelty and autonomy. Of course, we attempted, towards the end of the cinema chapter, to grapple with this problem, referring to a more complicated picture of connectedness between aesthetic forms, and to a movement between and across forms (the writer's self-reflexive use of language, cinematic moments of dramatization expressed by montage, the political-philosopher's concepts of 'money', 'cliché', 'break-flow' and so on) which emerged from our particular encounter with a cinematic text like *Boogie Nights*. And we suggested that it was potentially counter-productive to think of Deleuze as an unforgiving pedagogue or dogmatist: as a philosopher who privileges his own form of practice, even when, or for Rancière especially when, he seems on the surface to be attributing autonomy and novelty to a particular medium or art-form like cinema.

Two things follow from this discussion that are especially pertinent to us here. First, that a charge of dogmatism is immediately connected to an accusation of the privileging of philosophy vis-à-vis aesthetic form. Second, that the response to this charge implies that we develop a more general picture of the connectedness and intermingling of aesthetic forms. Taking the second point first, we can say that this gesture towards connectedness and intermingling of aesthetic forms presupposes that we can paint a more general picture of the function of the art-work, or as we shall prefer to put it, what happens in the art-work when we think of it as a dramatic event. Again we find ourselves anticipating an encounter with Deleuze and Guattari's more general discussion of the art-work in *What is Philosophy?* This, however, will become our focus later on in the chapter. Coming back to the first, and more urgent, point about the problem of the privileging of philosophy over art, it is important at this juncture to underline just how resolutely and stubbornly problematic this problem is. Indeed, we shall see that both Deleuze and Badiou (and here Badiou's critique of Deleuze can be turned back on him), in trying to fight the battle against dogmatism and empiricism, continually face this danger or problem when trying to think about events. This we will call the problem of *philosophism*; the privileging of philosophy when another discipline is better placed to make sense of the problematic phenomenon.

Deleuze: what happened?

A playwright is sitting outside a Paris café (it might be May '68) when something happens that catches her attention. Something has differentiated itself from the mass of other things that have happened in front of her: an exchange on the street, something funny, absurd, tragic; something she can't quite fathom. Her notebook, always to hand, is now filled with ideas – talk, scenery, directions, dialogue, costumes and such like tumble out on to the pages of her notebook as her coffee gets cold. Whatever it was that happened, she is now distilling the experience; characters are being formed, back-stories are emerging, all to bring that moment into vivid relief. She then takes these notes and transforms them into a script, a play-text. Maybe the characters from the street appear, or maybe only the feelings those characters created within her appear. A story emerges or maybe the constraints of story-telling have been forsaken in pursuit of a more abstract approach to whatever happened outside the café. In due course, the play is performed; the already dramatized moment is further dramatized. In this dramatization the moment outside the café is brought to life: the forces dormant within the script are roused by actors, directors, and set-designers; by the texture of the spoken word and the atmospherics of setting. On opening night, in front of the audience, all the elements that made a drama out of the dramatic event outside the café are brought to fruition as a live event.

We might imagine, if all the elements come together to make what we typically call 'good drama', that for our playwright there's a moment of discovery. Dramatization has helped her discover something about what happened outside the café because it has heightened that moment, condensed it, stretched it, enveloped and unfolded it in so many ways. At which point she may well feel like the moment has been redeemed and her work finished. Until five years later, with a new cast, a different director, in a new city, in the wake of a political crisis, she discovers something new, something unexpected in the dramatic moment once again. Whatever she thought had happened that day outside the café she now realizes that it was something else. Indeed, she now realizes that each time the play is performed this sense of re-evaluation may return because to dramatize the script is never simply to discover its essence and the essence of whatever happened but to create the forces that animate the script with each performance in a way that does not foreclose what happened. Each performance could be a new discovery. At which point, she realizes that it is no longer clear what happened.

As we saw in chapters two and three, Deleuze insists that we can encounter philosophical texts as if they were literary texts or play-scripts to be animated anew each time they are performed within another text. He considered concepts to be characters that could be brought to life to discover their force and that each time they are brought together on the stage of another's ideas they would be brought to life differently. Staging philosophical concepts in this way meant writing philosophy with the aim of tracing the dynamic trajectories of concepts – their path through texts, through a philosopher's system, but also outside of that system – as one would trace the arc of a character's journey through the play and how that impinges upon us. To repeat one of the key arguments from his defence of *Difference and Repetition*: 'given any concept, we can discover its drama, and the concept would never be divided or specified in a world of representation without the dramatic dynamisms that thus determine it in a material system beneath all possible representation' (Deleuze, 2004, 93). Therefore, analyzing concepts in this way must imply that their meaning will differ with each presentation; each enactment of a concept could, potentially, differ depending upon the textual context in which it emerged, the social and political environment within which it is staged, and so on. This, of course, relates to the liveness of thought, of making an event of thought. To restate the claim simply: philosophy, to the extent that it is animated by the method of dramatization, must become a live event.

The ontological presuppositions behind the method of dramatization were obviously the focus of an extended discussion in chapter three. But a few salient points are worth reiterating now. Dramatization is a method for the determination of (actual) concepts, where determination refers to a process of activating the (virtual) conditions that give those concepts their force and quality. These virtual conditions are what Deleuze repeatedly calls 'the idea' that conditions the concept. The idea is to be understood as a system of differential relations, not as an abstract form or mental phenomenon, where the differential relations themselves are the result of a distribution of singularities. Deleuze refers to these singularities as 'ideal events'. Dramatization, therefore, is a way of accessing the events that determine concepts – as every concept, to the extent that it has meaning at all, expresses an event that has already happened. In a crucial sense, of course, it is in the accessing of the event that we encounter its liveness; that is to say, the actual concept must be made into an event, made differently as a happening, in order to access it. As is well known, Deleuze often referred this process as 'counter-actualization'. In *Logic of Sense* we find this account:

> The role played [by an actor] is never that of a character; it is a theme (the complex theme or sense) constituted by the components of the event, that is, by the communicating singularities effectively liberated from the limits of individuals and persons...The actor thus

actualizes the event, but in a way that is entirely different from the actualization of the event in the depth of things. Or, rather, the actor redoubles this cosmic, or physical actualization, in his own way, which is singularly superficial – but because of it more distinct, trenchant and pure. Thus, the actor delimits the original, disengages from it an abstract line, and keeps from the event only its contour and splendour, becoming the actor of one's own events – a counter-actualization. (Deleuze, 1990, 150)

A number of the key elements of the method of dramatization we developed in the first part of the book are concisely captured and re-staged in this passage: counter-actualization requires the redistribution of the singularities of an idea; that is, a redistribution of the spatial-temporal dynamisms that constitute the idea. Redistribution, in this sense, is an intensification of the dynamisms that constitute the idea. Intensification is a change in the intensive, virtual, relationships between the singularities. This can only be achieved by a creative experimentalism akin to the actor's experimentation with the themes of the character's 'journey' – a mode of experimentation with ideas that is both a theoretical and a practical activity. Put simply, something has to happen, there has to be the constitution of an event, in order to experiment with whatever the events of the character's life mean.

However, what this passage also allows us to begin to bring into focus is the problematic nature of Deleuze's method of dramatization, particularly when we think of it as a means for the determination of concepts. This is the case because we can see that the event that conditions the concept can only be 'discovered' by instituting an event or happening that is 'entirely different' from the actualization of the conditioning event, itself to be found 'in the depth of things'. Despite being entirely different, Deleuze suggests that these events are nonetheless related to each other. How are they related? Unfortunately, the language Deleuze uses to discuss this relation is not always clear: in this passage it includes 'redoubling', 'delimiting' and 'disengaging' in order to follow the 'contour and splendour' of the original event. All of which is consistent with the processes of different/ciation – actualization and counter-actualization – that he presents in *Difference and Repetition* (Deleuze, 1994, 208ff). And yet we are still left asking the following question: how can counter-actualization express the event 'in the depth of things' if it is itself an event that happens to constitute a difference.

Back at the café our playwright wonders if the productions that have followed from her original experience have anything to do with the experience itself: has she really discovered anything at all? Is what happened still mysterious?

Badiou: getting to the truth of what happened

It is this persistent sense of the mysterious nature of the relation between events that gives Badiou's critique of Deleuze much of its weight (Badiou, 1994; 2000; 2004; 2009). The best expression of this critique is in *Logics of Worlds*, in the section 'The Event According to Deleuze' (Badiou, 2009, 381–7). In this section, Badiou draws out four axioms of the Deleuzean event from *Logic of Sense*, which he contrasts with alternatives of his own, so as to 'obtain a pretty good axiomatic for what I call "event"';

1. 'Unlimited-becoming becomes the event itself.' Badiou is drawing attention to the fact that Deleuze treats the event as an intensification in the line of life, the eternal becoming of all forms of existence. The Deleuzean event, according to Badiou, is therefore 'the becoming of becoming'. He contrasts this with an axiom of his own: the event is a 'pure cut in becoming' by which he means that events are moments when the 'inexistent' comes into existence. As such, there is no vital continuity but an excessive eruption from a condition of utter lack.
2. 'A life is composed of the same single Event, despite all the variety of what happens to it.' The unlimited-becoming Badiou detects in Deleuze's philosophy of the event leads him to argue that, for Deleuze, all events are expressions of one Event; the 'eventum tantum' of *Logic of Sense*. Badiou's alternative axiom is that all events are 'separate' from other events. Declaring that Deleuze's idea of the resonance between events has 'no charm' for him, Badiou characterizes events as the 'dull and utterly unresonant sound' that brings nothing into harmony.
3. 'The nature of the event is other than that of the actions and passions of the body. But it results from them.' Badiou is pointing out that for Deleuze events affect bodies but not directly, as this process of affect must take place through the mediator of bodies without organs; virtual/actual bodies that mediate between ideal virtual events and actual bodies or states of affairs. In contrast, Badiou claims that it is the eruption of an event which becomes incorporated within subjectivizable bodies. Where Deleuze, he claims, treats bodies and events as of different orders, Badiou treats bodies as the result of events.

4. 'The event is always what has just happened, what will happen but
   never what is happening.' This is the crucial axiom that crystallizes the problem with dramatic events. How can we account for the
   drama in dramatic events if we have to stage it differently in order
   to discover it? The Deleuzean event resides in the past and it can
   only be discovered from the perspective of an event in the future
   that leaves the presence of the event, its drama, mysterious. Badiou
   suggests, for his part, that the event is always 'an atemporal instant
   which disjoins the previous state of an object (the site) from its subsequent state'. And, the event 'presents us with the present' (Badiou,
   2009, 384).

It is our view that Badiou has identified a number of pressing problems with Deleuze's pre-occurrence theory of event and the method
of dramatization that accompanies it. Of course, we need hardly agree
with all these criticisms, and various Deleuze scholars have challenged
Badiou's critical interpretation, both in its generality and it details
(Widder, 2001; Smith 2003; Williams, 2009). For us, though, Badiou
has pinpointed an important difficulty Deleuze has in accounting for
a sense of being in the moment when something dramatic happens.
Deleuze's pre-occurrence approach to the significance of the event is
problematic to the extent that it robs his theory of one of the markers
of events: the presence of drama, the moment outside the café. But we
also know that Badiou is resistant to the idea that the meaning of events
could be simply located in their appearance and the experience we have
of them. Given the concerns he shares with Deleuze regarding the location of significance within the event, and his criticism of the Deleuzean
alternative, namely that events have their significance in the past as it
becomes re-staged in the future, it becomes clear why Badiou turns to a
post-occurrence theory of the significance of the event. It is not clear,
however, that he overcomes the problem he finds in Deleuze.

In *Being and Event* Badiou discusses how historical events appear from
within natural situations (Badiou, 2005a, 173–77). In order for events to
emerge from situations, the situation must contain within it 'an evental
site'. This is a multiple present within the situation that is not represented within the situation. In a rare moment of reprieve for the reader
of *Being and Event*, Badiou gives an image of what this means. He discusses a family living together, going on holiday together, etc. each of
whose members is fully represented, that is registered, within and by
the state. If we imagine, he goes on, that there is a 'clandestine' member
of this family, tied by blood so to speak, but not a member in the sense

that he or she does not belong to the family, engage in family activities and is not registered by the state as belonging to the family, then this member is present in the family situation but not represented within it. Hallward provides an interesting gloss: 'an evental site ... is certainly in a situation, but it belongs to it as something uncertain, something whose own contents remain indiscernible and mysterious, if not sinister and threatening' (Hallward, 2003, 120). This clandestine and mysterious presence in the situation is the condition for the emergence of an historical event that will shake the foundations of the natural situation.

While the evental site presents the conditions for an atemporal cut through becoming by virtue of the non-presentation of a (clandestinely present) multiple in the representational field of the situation, this is not enough in itself to constitute an event. For the inexistent multiple to become an event there must be an intervention (Badiou, 2005a, 201–211). Intervention, according to Badiou, is neither the interpretation nor the glorification of the clandestine but its naming: 'identifying that there has been some indecidability, and in deciding its belonging to the situation' (Badiou, 2005a, 202). As Badiou recognizes, however, the real difficulty is not in naming the event but in 'following the consequences of an event' (Badiou, 2005a, 211). It is this notion of following the consequences of the naming of the clandestine that leads Badiou to claim that an event is properly constituted by being faithful to the intervention. This fidelity is such that it is embodied in subjects who maintain and sustain the truth of their designation for what has happened. Fidelity thereby constitutes subjects as militants of the intervention and the truth to which they adhere is the naming of the unnamable and mysterious clandestine individuals of the situation.

The mysterious nature of what happened according to the Deleuzean schema of the event and its dramatization is replaced with a faith in the naming of the un-nameable in what happened so as to establish the truth of the event. Whatever happened outside the café that day, our playwright must declare the un-nameable nameable and then remain faithful to that truth. In this way, the event is guaranteed after the event, so to speak. At which point we appear to have reached a similar problem to that which we encountered with Deleuze; the moment of the event itself, its drama, is occluded (in this case) by a post-occurrence theory of where that drama must ultimately reside. While Badiou has criticized Deleuze for not accounting for the present moment of the event as the cut between the past and future, he can only account for it himself by treating the present moment of the event as that which contains a mysterious inexistent multiple, that only comes-to-be when the fidelity to the name is held as a truth. Deleuze's *absent* present, which in turn leads to the mysteries of an ever-present event, is replaced, on Badiou's account, by an *empty* present which in turn is filled by an ever-present faith in an act of naming a mysteriously inexistent presence. Either way, the present seems to disappear in the ever-present.

This schism regarding the presence of dramatic events is a useful perspective through which to view the 'debate' between Deleuze (and Guattari) and Badiou. When Deleuze and Guattari take Badiou to task in *What is Philosophy?*, for all that they recognize the 'particularly interesting undertaking' he is engaged in, they claim that he misconstrues the nature of events by not recognizing that every event is already a mixture of states of affairs (the given situation, in Badiou's terms) and virtual events. Because Badiou's events appear as a cut in becoming, Deleuze and Guattari imply, they do not actually appear at all; they are lacking in reality because they do not appear 'beside', 'against', 'face to face, or back to back' vis-à-vis the actual/situation. For Deleuze and Guattari, the presence of the dramatic event disappears because it is an error to think that one can separate the event from the state of affairs that expresses it (on this point, see Lecercle 1999b; 2010).

In our view, however, Deleuze's pre-occurrence theory of the event does not seem to fare much better because it risks creating a similar distance between the philosophical search for meaning and the experience of dramatic events. In Deleuze's absent present and Badiou's empty present of the event, the drama seems to get lost. The root problem for both Deleuze and Badiou when thinking about events is that they hesitate to address the dramatic event itself, the moment of drama so to speak, because of the dual dangers of empiricism and dogmatism. However, this, as we have seen, leads both thinkers away from the moment in search of a philosophical source for the significance of events that does not tie that meaning to the paradoxical nature of what happens when events happen. Both require that the event must have an actual and present moment to it but both diminish the experience of being involved in dramatic events. But the problem of dramatic events remains. So a key question reasserts itself, but in hopefully a clearer or more refined form: can the drama of dramatic events be theorized from the inside while avoiding both the traps of empiricism and dogmatism? And, going forward with our more particular concern here; does the method of dramatization we have been developing in conjunction with Deleuze and Guattari remain, given the problems we have identified above, a useful methodological tool or way of thinking about dramatic events?

Some thing is happening

Leaving aside, for the moment, the broader question concerning the method of dramatization, let us return to *les événements*, and, in particular, a rather revealing account that Badiou gives of what it is like to be inside such a dramatic event:

> If we add up the anecdotes one by one, we can always say that at any given moment there were actors, certain people who provoked this or that result. But the crystallization of all those moments, their generalization, and then the way in which everyone was caught up in it, was well beyond what any one person might have thought possible – that's what I call an evental dimension. (Hallward, 2003, 123)

The importance of this more personal and reflective account of *les événements* is that it captures something that gets lost in Badiou's post-occurrence theory of the truth of what happened. In particular, the *sensation* of being involved in something happening exceeds our capacity to *think* about what it is that one is involved in. Thinking returns as the decision is made to name this sensation and follow the consequences of the intervention as it assumes the form of a truth-procedure. But this truth is always the truth of the name not the sensation. Put like this, therefore, our problem of trying to accord dramatic events significance (at least, part of the problem) is of the order of sensation rather than thought. The danger of this appeal to sensation, however, is that it may lead directly back to the traps of either empiricism or dogmatism: either we can merely describe the sensation of being involved in a dramatic event by describing how it felt to the individuals involved or immersed in the contingencies of the situation; or, we presume, regardless of how individuals describe it, that the significance of what they felt is given by the pre-ordained essence of the event. Such is the provocation of Deleuze's and Badiou's respective philosophies of the event. However, in trying to ward-off the dual dangers of empiricism and dogmatism, both Deleuze and Badiou remain wedded to the idea of a philosophical solution to the problem of dramatic events. The danger now is that the drama incorporated within the dramatic event remains occluded by virtue of being subordinated to its role as a bearer of being or truth. It is in this sense, then, that both Deleuze and Badiou (in the particular respects outlined above) encounter the trap of *philosophism*. And by 'philosophism' we mean the following: the tendency to accord philosophy a privileged role vis-à-vis other disciplines in the designation of experience.

The dangers associated with philosophism are not lost on Deleuze (and Guattari) and Badiou. For instance, Deleuze and Guattari implicitly and explicitly warned against using art for philosophical purposes and sought instead to find the concepts proper to the aesthetic forms they engaged with. Indeed, and as we saw in chapter two, during the period of collaboration begun by *Anti-Oedipus*, Deleuze and Guattari sought time and again to locate various aesthetic forms at the heart of their philosophy of difference, attributing to these forms a particular power or autonomy to dramatically effect movements in (political) thought. By the time of their final work, *What is Philosophy?*, this belief in the autonomy of aesthetic forms had hardened into the strict separation of philosophy and the art-work. Turning to Badiou, it is clear that he also is concerned to distinguish philosophy from art and other disciplines ('science', 'politics' and 'love') with the aim of warding-off any lurking philosophical imperialism. He argues, indeed, that 'philosophy is under the conditions of art, science, politics and love, but it is always damaged, wounded, serrated by the evental and singular character of these conditions' (Badiou, 2003, 101).

For all this, neither Deleuze (and Guattari) nor Badiou specifically address the excess of sensation that defines the experience of being in a dramatic event; drawn, as they are, either to the underlying sense or the overarching truth of the sensation itself. The drama in the experience of dramatic events, they both imply, must signal something else of significance: this is the attitude of the philosopher, their shared philosophism. Of course, Deleuze and Badiou are philosophers par excellence so this charge hardly seems appropriate: it's just what they do as philosophers, is it not? Moreover, in separating philosophy from other disciplines or from its conditions, they share the desire to save philosophy from its destruction through absorption by other disciplines: Deleuze and Guattari's *What is Philosophy?* and Badiou's *Manifesto for Philosophy* are two of the great texts in defence of philosophy to have come out of the twentieth century. As such, it may appear churlish to criticize them for being too philosophical! But this is not our point or concern here. Rather, it is their shared tendency, despite their shared recognition of what we are calling philosophism, to recognize the drama in dramatic events only to treat it as absent or empty with regard to locating the significance of what happened outside of the event itself. And, returning to the method of dramatization, if we cannot find a satisfactory way of locating the drama as it unfolds within the dramatic event, then the method remains too abstract. That is to say, we forgo the possibility of having some kind of direct experience that has a significance that is intrinsic to the moment of dramatization as it occurs. At this point, our earlier question returns, with an added dimension: is it possible to articulate the experience of being wrapped up in dramatic events while avoiding the traps of empiricism, dogmatism and philosophism?

A clue to an answer to this question is given in a letter written by Deleuze and Guattari regarding the legacies of May '68. In it they say that 'the event creates a new existence' (Deleuze, 2006, 234). Before it has either sense or truth, an event brings something into existence. This is crucial: while it is true to say that *something has happened*, what has happened is that *some thing has come into existence*. Far from being the site of an absent or empty significance the dramatic event is full of some 'newly existing thing'. What is it that is brought into existence? This cannot be answered at the level of representation, as that will depend upon the state of affairs or the situation into which an event intervenes. Or, to put it another way, it would be a mistake to say that it is always the same 'thing' that comes into existence. At the level of the pre-representational, however, we can borrow from Deleuze and Guattari an insightful way of talking about what happens when new things come into existence. This brings us finally, then, to an encounter with their general aesthetics, their wide-ranging discussion of art-work, as developed in *What is Philosophy?* (Deleuze and Guattari, 1994, 163–199).

As is well known, Deleuze and Guattari speak in broad or general terms that an art-work preserves something of its moment of creation within itself: not the artist's intention, or labour, but the 'bloc of sensations' that it expresses (Deleuze and Guattari, 1994, 163–64). This 'bloc of sensations' is 'a compound of percepts and affects' distinct from the perceptions of the perceiver and the affections of those affected. It is a 'bloc' of sensations, therefore, because it is not simply some *thing* that some *one* then senses; it is a structured domain of intensity in which thing and person (the animal and its environment, the cinematic apparatus and a spectator, language and its user etc) are implicated. Put like this, we see no reason why the dramatic event cannot be described as a work of art. This brings us to an ever more refined version of the problem animating this final chapter: from a philosophical perspective, the problem with dramatic events is that they *are* works of art. Of course, this is not a problem if one assumes that this makes dramatic events 'an art object' capable of being incorporated with an aesthetic discourse. But to de-problematize dramatic events in this way would simply be to reinstate the philosophism that we earlier criticized. If we wish to avoid this philosophism, and we do, then it is better to retain the problematic nature of dramatic events from a philosophical point of view and then to consider the consequences that follow from thinking outside of this perspective.

It is worth underscoring that this suggestion, though drawn from *What is Philosophy?*, still sits in a problematic relationship to Deleuze's philosophy of the event. Further, it could be seen as dislocating the relationship between Deleuze's and Badiou's respective theories of the event, particularly if we think of them in terms of an emphasis on continuity versus cut. For if, as we claim, the drama in dramatic events can and must be presented in a direct and intrinsic experience (what Deleuze and Guattari call the 'being of sensation' that emerges in a structured domain of intensity) and that this can be achieved if the drama is treated as a work of art (rather than as an object to be used in the philosophical search for significance) then the dramatic event qua art-work cuts open being and in doing so will condition any philosophical conceptualization of (the sense or truth) of that which has come into existence. This may well irritate Deleuzeans and Badiouians alike: the Deleuzean will recognize that the construction of concepts is being made subordinate to the production of works of art: the Badiouian that the conditions of philosophy are being reduced from four to one. That said, our playwright may well recognize that the problem with dramatic events is only a problem for philosophers; for her, the drama of being in a dramatic event was that of being a part of a work of art and her play can be treated as simply another work of art, both standing alone, both having an autonomy expressed through the being of the sensations that emerge within the domain of their unfolding.

Passing over into sensation or abstraction?

Of course, we realize that making a claim on behalf of an artist (whether imagined or real) against the dangers of philosophical imperialism is still a provocation. The provocation being that this is merely the reassertion of that imperialism, but under the cover of a new name. We argued above that the problem of viewing dramatic events as works of art mysteriously disappears if, or as soon as, we recalibrate them as 'art objects' which are then subject to an aesthetic discourse or words that clothe and smother, that smother by clothing. The reader has a right to be worried that there simply may be, as Jacques Rancière puts it, 'too many words' that 'comment' on aesthetic practices, words which 'devour it' (Rancière, 2007, 70). In this concluding part of the chapter it will prove useful to bring Rancière briefly back into the picture, a picture that may get a little more complicated because of his presence.

We should already have a sense of the nature of this complication from Rancière's critique of Deleuze's cinematic modernism outlined in the previous chapter. And this critique can now be broadened to include his and Guattari's general aesthetics (Rancière, 2009, 73–74) as well as Badiou's thinking on art (Rancière, 2004, 218–31). The general form of this critique comes by way of a Rancièrian concern or paradox that should be familiar by now: namely, that the philosopher-pedagogue seems to invest the art-work with an autonomy that robs it of autonomy. As he rather pointedly and caustically says in his discussion of the art-work in *What is Philosophy?*; 'The very thing that makes the aesthetic "political" stands in the way of all strategies for politicizing art' (Rancière, 2009, 73–74). That is to say, the philosopher claims no hierarchy exists between her or his disciplinary practice and aesthetic practices, suggesting that what happens in the latter is its own autonomous preserve. But what the philosopher often fails to appreciate is that the linguistic currency of these investments in aesthetic autonomy (where currency here can be read as the philosophical meta-language that is downloaded onto art-works, whether a Badiouian idea of 'Inaesthetics', the Deleuze-Guattarian notion of the 'being of sensation', or whatever else) are such that they bear no real significance on what actually happens in aesthetic practices of various sorts. From this Rancièrian perspective, perhaps the real danger of philosophism is neither wrongly clothing nor unfairly devouring, but that it remains standing alone, living in abstraction, trying to trade on a currency that has no worth as such.

So not only does Rancière pose a difficulty to philosophers such as Badiou and Deleuze (and Guattari) in a manner that we could find interesting, provocative and indeed useful, he also, potentially, implicates our own argument which rests, you will recall, on the following possibility: namely, retaining the idea of the problematic nature of dramatic events from a philosophical point of view and then considering the consequences that follow from thinking outside this perspective. And we have suggested that this entails an aestheticizing move whereby philosophism is met head-on by the notion of the dramatic event as a work of art that stands alone, that has some kind of autonomy to cut open being (to bring something new into existence) in ways that condition any philosophical meta-language that would then seek to attribute concepts to it. But, again, the question then reasserts itself: have we simply replaced philosophism with a form of aestheticism, a new philosophism in everything but name?

Restaging a potentially Rancièrian critique in this way is a useful reminder about the persistently problematic nature of philosophism, a problem that cannot be conceptually wished away or dealt with by easy or quick investments in aesthetic autonomy. Now, the linguistic currency of our investment in aesthetic autonomy is clearly more Deleuze-Guattarian than Badiouian, as the idea of the art-work 'standing alone' is very much Deleuze and Guattari's explicit concern in *What is Philosophy?* When thinking about dramatic events the key, for us at least, is not to utilize the imagery that Deleuze and Guattari evoke when they talk about art-works as the opportunity for a quick philosophical investment: here their words become subject to logics analogous to product branding, public relations, and before we know it 'marketing appears as the concept itself' (Deleuze and Guattari, 1994, 146). Against this kind of interpretation, and clearly in line with the method of dramatization as we have been developing it, it is crucial to encounter Deleuze and Guattari's words for their aesthetic provocation, their dramatic effects. This, of course, was one of the key points that we made in the language chapter. Indeed, it was a crucial aspect of our rejoinder to the Rancièrian and Badiouian critiques in the cinema chapter; namely, that they rested too contentedly in their view that Deleuze (and Guattari) are philosophical pedagogues, rather than seeing them as dramatists bringing concepts to life. And, now, as we head toward a conclusion, it is worth trying to recapture or re-emphasize the significance of this approach to Deleuze and Guattari's work.

To be sure, Deleuze and Guattari (and indeed Badiou), despite all their protestations otherwise, can be viewed as philosophers whose pedagogical paternalism can be subject to critical scrutiny. But this, rather caustic, reading is itself limited (and this means that our critical remarks in relation to Badiou, Deleuze and Guattari in this chapter, and indeed throughout the book, are also to some degree implicated in this context) to the extent that it becomes fixated on viewing the philosopher's words only from the point of view of some supposedly didactic-conceptual function. However, if we open ourselves up to an encounter with the words Deleuze and Guattari particularly use in their discussion of how the art-work should and can 'stand up on its own' in a text like *What is Philosophy?*, we can potentially experience something else; something else can happen. Again, we find ourselves coming back to stressing the significance of the performative and self-consciously creative or writerly form of Deleuze and Guattari's philosophy, how their arguments can produce effects of various sorts. So, for instance, rather than reading Deleuze and Guattari as philosophers working in abstraction to construct a modernist canon of art-works in *What is Philosophy?* we might want to view them (once again in line with Lecercle's suggestion), as 'literary modernists', artists or dramatists practicing 'philosophy as a kind of writing, with a vengeance' (Lecercle, 2010, 128).

And with Lecercle's suggestive remarks in mind, it is worth turning to the first few sentences in chapter seven of *What is Philosophy?* where Deleuze and Guattari begin to dramatize and to capture the sense that the art-work has an autonomy or a capacity to stand up alone. They write:

> The young man will smile for as long as the canvas lasts. Blood throbs under the skin of a woman's face, the wind shakes a branch, a group of men prepare to leave. In a novel or a film, the young man will stop smiling, but he will start smiling again when we turn to this page or that moment. Art preserves, and it is the only thing in the world that is preserved... The young girl maintains the pose that she has had for five thousand years, a gesture that no longer depends on whoever made it. The air still has the turbulence, the gust of wind, and the light that it had that day last year, and it no longer depends on whoever was breathing it that morning. If art preserves it does not do so like industry, by adding a substance to make a thing last. The thing became independent of its "model" from the start... And it is no less independent of the viewer or hearer... What about the creator? It is independent of the creator through the self-positing of the created, which is preserved in itself. What is preserved – the thing or the work of art – is *a bloc of sensations, that is to say, a compound of affects and percepts.* (Deleuze and Guattari, 1994, 163–64)

As we pointed out earlier, the 'bloc of sensations' that Deleuze and Guattari's words here evoke is what the art-work is said to preserve in itself. The art-work stands up on its own to the extent that it remains 'independent' or autonomous from its creator, from its potential audience, from its material situation, and even from the medium or form in and through which it is expressed. Something happens in the art-work, something new is created, a cut in being, the structuring of a domain of intensity. Now, the question of whether Deleuze and Guattari's words in the passage above merely attribute concepts ('bloc of sensations', 'affects and percepts') to explain what supposedly happens when art-works are created, or the question of whether their words and philosophical meta-language or meta-narrative ('art as the being of sensation') are actually the creative force which shapes or mediates our sense of the art-work in advance and in the abstract, can, of course, be questions framed in caustically critical terms, but there is nothing necessary or indeed productive in this. For what if we were to say that, yes, the creative force and dramatic impact of Deleuze and Guattari's words shapes or gives rise to a particular sensory experience or sensation, but that here the power of their words immediately expresses the sense of something dramatic that is brought into existence (say, problems or questions concerning how we can possibly have a smile without a bodily form, or the five thousand year pose, or an image of aesthetic creation that is somehow different to, or autonomous from, 'industry' and so on) and that this then can be experienced as a cut in being, as something that has happened. Could we not say that Deleuze and Guattari's own literary and creative use of language performs a dramatizing function, whereby their words always-already have the potential to directly pass over into a sensation? 'The writer's specific materials', say Deleuze and Guattari, 'are words and syntax that...passes into sensation' (Deleuze and Guattari, 1994, 167).

Conclusion

At the beginning of the book we speculated about the broader implications that could be said to follow from the establishment and defence of a Deleuze–Guattarian method of dramatization, even suggesting possible future lines of enquiry, or some contexts and ways in which the method could be further put to work. Indeed, in the latter part of the book, we began to put the method to work in the context of a discussion about the nature of language, cinema and the significance of events. We would like, by way of conclusion, to provide three propositions that, to our minds, help further crystallize some important implications of the method as we have developed it. Our hope is that these propositions are read, at least in part, as stage directions, slogans even, that can be used, abused, and performed anew by creative reader-actors. Needless to say, this list of propositions is hardly exhaustive, and there is no way we would want to begin to try to predict how the method of dramatization will get picked up and used (if at all). But we nonetheless offer the following as a series of suggestive remarks that indicate how we think the method could be put to work in the future.

Philosophers have only interpreted the world, the point is to dramatize it!

In chapter two, we situated Deleuze and Guattari's method of dramatization in relation to Marx's famous thesis eleven (McLellan, 2000, 173). Like Marx, Deleuze and Guattari work with a concept of change that has a distinct epistemological resonance. We know the world through changing it. We acquire or access knowledge about the political world (i.e., political concepts) through the activity of making it different. Of course, 'changing it' or 'making it different' here means 'dramatizing it', and dramatizing it in a way that holds the normative implications of its particular dramatic unfolding in suspense. In important respects, Deleuze and Guattari are heirs to a critical tradition that is in turn shaped by a resolutely modern philosophical method: the Cartesian spirit or assumption that a sound and rigorous method is one that can help us distinguish knowledge about the political world from the mere opinions that may operate or circulate through it. Clearly, this gets complicated in Deleuze and Guattari as knowledge becomes a practical activity that sets in motion all settled dualisms (including, needless to say, 'knowledge' versus the 'doxa') through the process of intensification that Deleuze called dramatization.

And by holding in suspense the normative implications that follow from the practicing of the method of dramatization, Deleuze and Guattari's political philosophy sits in a stubbornly and persistently critical relationship to the dominant mode of doing political philosophy; namely, the doing of normative or moral philosophy (again we have very much in mind the communicative turns that animate and encircle so much of contemporary liberal political thought). Indeed, and as we suggested at the end of the first chapter, the method of dramatization directs us to an interrogation of the dominant disciplinary modes and critical methodologies of political thought. And it is obviously in light of this broader impulse that our critical interrogation of Habermas undertaken in chapter one is to be viewed. But this is only one example of a particular critical reading (focusing, you will recall, on how Habermas's argument for the priority of communicative action got dramatized and brought to life by way of a linguistic or rhetorical form that restaged it, paradoxically, as a series of strategic and non-negotiable 'order-words' or imperatives) one potential use of the method among many others.

Rather than putting the method to work in order to interrogate critically the dramatizing strategies of contemporary political theorists of influence (whether Habermas, Taylor, or Berlin, to mention a few others that figured briefly in our discussions previously), we could turn our attention to the history of philosophy and political thought. And rather than focusing very specifically on the literary and rhetorical style of political theorists (as we did in our analysis of texts such as *The Theory of Communicative Action* and *Moral Consciousness and Communicative Action*) we could think, for example, about the way political thought gets dramatized in relation to emerging media, cultural, or technological forms. This, of course, is one of Deleuze's concerns in the cinema books we discussed in chapter five, a crucial problem or question raised by his cinematic modernism; namely, how does the emergence of cinema as a medium or technological form shape, or even engender, thinking? Now, the history of Western thought (political and otherwise) is replete with examples of how new, or emerging, technological forms' impact on it and bring it to life. For example, we could go back to the Cartesian method and look again, say, at how Descartes' concept of perception brings into play the developing technology of optics and lens-based media. For instance, when Descartes seems to suggest the possibility that perceived objects can and 'do imprint very perfect images on the back of our eyes' he does so by making the following connection:

> Some people have very ingeniously explained this...by comparison with the images that appear in a chamber, when having it completely closed except for a single hole, and having put in front of this hole a glass in the form of a lens, we stretch behind, at a specific distance, a white cloth on which the light that comes from the objects outside forms these images. For they say that this chamber represents the eye; this hole, the pupil; this lens, ...all those parts of the parts of the eye that cause refraction; and this cloth, the interior membrane....
> (Descartes, 2001, 100)

By foregrounding the relation between developing thought and developing technological, media, cultural, aesthetic forms in this way, the method of dramatization can orient us to a series of research questions and problems that tend not to be at the forefront of the minds of scholars working in the history of political thought. As we have implicitly and explicitly argued throughout the book, putting the method of dramatization to work means that we take very seriously the idea that the very formulation of concepts is conditioned and dramatized in and though a variety of forms and genres; that (political) concepts come to us from a range of places, and that a critical sensitivity to this is a crucial acknowledgement of the openness and pluralism of political thought itself. This brings us neatly to our second proposition.

Political Theory is not the pursuit of an exclusive minority!

For us, one of the most immediate and obvious ways of thinking about the openness and pluralism of political thought is to begin to reflect on how political concepts get dramatized all around us. As we said in chapter one, the dramatization of political concepts is densely woven into the fabric of everyday life. And if political theory is an activity that presupposes the creation of political concepts whose purpose is to help us access the domain of the political, then it can never be the occupation of an exclusive minority. Or, perhaps more accurately, if political theory is understood and practiced as though it is the property of an exclusive minority, then it is immediately impoverished and curtailed. Of course, this happens all the time; it is a constant danger. For state-funded academics like us there is the obvious problem of institutionalization and its attending dangers of abstraction (we become the product or commodity that the institution demands according to its own logic, a logic that often fails to connect in any significant way to the social and political world) and repression (the logics we follow operate precisely in a fashion that stop us from engaging in productive thought). Deleuze, in the following passage of *Dialogues*, says it all when he says:

> The history of philosophy has always been the agent of power in philosophy, and even in thought. It has played the represser's role: how can you think without having read Plato, Descartes, Kant and Heidegger, and so-and-so's book about them? A formidable school of intimidation...manufactures specialists in thought.... An image of thought called philosophy has been formed historically and it effectively stops people from thinking. (Deleuze and Parnet, 1987, 13)

It is striking the extent to which Deleuze's particular remarks here can be made to resonate through the culture industry that has inevitably grown up around his and Guattari's work. Can we begin to talk of a formidable school of intimidation in Deleuze and Guattari studies, the manufacture of specialists in Deleuze–Guattarian thought? Is it possible to think about the importance of Deleuze and Guattari's work without having read so-and-so's book about them, or the key figures in the history of philosophy that influenced them (Bergson, Spinoza, Nietzsche and so on ...)? These are persistently problematic tendencies and we do not pretend for one second to be immune to them. What we would say here, however, is that the exclusivist and parochial aspects of any given form of thinking (Deleuze–Guattarian or otherwise) will always get opened up through their dramatization; that is, in and through the ways in which concepts get brought to life. And during the course of the book we have obviously tried to make a play of this. On the one hand, we have done this by pointing to the resonant, provocative and engaging form in which Deleuze and Guattari think or, more particularly from our point of view, do political philosophy (hence the importance we placed in chapter four on Deleuze and Guattari's writing style, their use of humour and slogans and so on). And, on the other hand, we have stressed how their way of doing political thought, their method, can be put to work (hence the way in which we folded that discussion of humour and slogans into a particular analysis of Belfast as a post-conflict city).

Actually, it is worth returning to our discussion of Belfast in this context. For, as we emphasized, the concept of Belfast as a post-conflict city comes to us from a range of places and via a number of cultural and aesthetic forms. These, to repeat, include: commercial discourses relating to property development and urban regeneration, local and regional news media, television, film and architecture. Further, there is always the potential for an intermingling of forms here, a pluralism or series of media that can connect up in the conjuncture in particular ways. We could think, in this respect, about the public art and sculpture that has emerged in the city since the signing of the Good Friday Agreement in 1998. As built form, public art and sculpture immediately connects to the visual-cum-spatial grammar of architecture, but it also can do the work of urban regeneration, connecting, as it does, to the dominant commercial discourses and business interests that play through the development of the urban environment. As we discussed above, the notion of Belfast as a post-conflict city does its work in the social formation by operating as a promise: that we are seeing the emergence of a form of public life no longer primarily shaped by the antagonisms generated by political motivated violence. This promise functions normatively, gesturing, as it does, towards an ideal to which the city must move, rather than as a description of an actually existing state of affairs. How, then, does public art and sculpture figure here?

Public art in Belfast conceptualizes and politicizes the city precisely by expressing the desire for its de-politicization. By this we mean that it seeks to foster a de-politicization of public space, where 'de-politicization of public space' means the attempted neutralization of any lingering sectarian striations and the promotion of a smooth and welcoming space amenable to consumption (Dewesbury and Porter, 2010). This is particularly the case in the city-centre of Belfast, where the potential for neutralizing or smoothing out space is undoubtedly greater than in those other parts of the city that are still indelibly marked by a persistent and enduring sectarian striation (Shirlow and Murtagh, 2006). Two things are immediately worth bearing in mind when considering how public art functions in the city-centre of Belfast. First, there is the visual potential of public art to work as spectacle or icon, and (at least in terms of the commercial agenda of emphasizing how Belfast is a city open for business) public art in this context can function as a visual marker, or 'gateway', that informs potential consumer-citizens and consumer-tourists of their arrival in a city that is set up to meet their consumptive needs. Second, there is the architectural and geographical potential of public art to map public space in highly codified ways, or in accordance with a commercial logic of consumption. Put simply: public art in Belfast can, and indeed does, map a *retail circuit* (the notion of the 'retail circuit' figures prominently and strongly in current local and national discourses of governance and in the justifications for the public funding of public art-works in Belfast and in Northern Ireland more generally) for consumer-citizens and consumer-tourists, literally orienting them around in the city in the same way, say, that crowds of shoppers are directed in stores like IKEA.

So, while, on the one hand, we can think of public art as the smoothing out of public space, rendering it more amenable to consumption, this presupposes codifying, shaping, striating the space in particular ways, or in accordance with a logic of consumption. Rough with the smooth, we might say, as the patterning or striating movements that attend the desire for capital flow and accumulation (in this case, the desire for the contents of consumer's wallets to find their way into the shops in Belfast city-centre or, more broadly still, the desire for inward investment into the social-political formation) give rise to processes of smoothing; or, what Deleuze and Guattari would refer to as the emergence of 'smooth capital' (Deleuze and Guattari, 1988, 492).

Coming back to the implications that follow from the method of dramatization, our point in referring again to Belfast is a suggestive, and hopefully, simple one. For while we, as political theorists, could write a political theory of contemporary 'post-conflict' Belfast (its ideology of consumption, the role that property developers and business interests have played in 'normalizing', remaking or smoothing out the city and so on), nothing for us more forcefully dramatizes the concept of Belfast as a post-conflict city than its developing built environment and form, whether public art, or domestic and commercial property development. So in order to write this political theory, and in order to write it better, with more forceful purpose, vitality and resonant power, it would undoubtedly be productive for us to also take a walk around and orient ourselves in Belfast to see how the notion of the 'post-conflict' city is being conceptualized within the shifting spaces of urban and property-commercial development. As Deleuze and Guattari were often fond of saying, going out for a stroll and experiencing a little wind from the outside can be productive, and we think political theorists like us (and, dare we say it, like you too) need to get out more. This brings us to our final proposition.

Make political philosophy an event or, what amounts to the same thing, an art-work!

As we said in chapter three, there is nothing in being a professional, state-funded, thinker that privileges such individuals when it comes to the dramatization of political concepts. If the political thinker, the political philosopher, is to become, in Deleuze and Guattari's phrasing, the 'friend of the concept', then she needs to be willing to *make an event of thought*. This, of course, is a slogan that we have used throughout the book, and the concept of the event gets its most detailed treatment in chapter six. What do we now have to say on the matter, particularly as we move towards our conclusion? Well, we wish simply to reiterate the importance of thinking the event in relation to the art-work. For us, there is no reason why we cannot describe the activity of doing political philosophy, the dramatization of political concepts, in aesthetic terms. Political philosophy preserves something in the moment of its creation, a sensation or series of sensations, a structured domain of intensity. This structured domain of intensity or series of sensations is intrinsic to the moment(s) of its dramatic unfolding, what we have been calling a 'dramatic event'. So if we took our own advice and decided to take a walk around Belfast in order to get a feel or an experience of how the post-conflict city is being dramatized in and through the shifting spaces of urban and property-commercial development, then we would need to be alive to how this experience would be intrinsic to what it is that happens to us in those moments when we are traversing the city. Of course, we could only speculate about the particular significance of this (whether we might be charmed by an experience of the 'retail circuit' that plays into a desire to think of Belfast as a city that has moved on from a more troubled past, or, conversely, whether the smoothness of this consumptive experience might precipitate depressing thoughts concerning the city's homogenization and conformity with flows of global capital), but a general point remains: we only know, access, politically conceptualize, the city in the moments of its dramatization as such, only when they pass over into sensation(s).

In an important sense, then, we are saying that political philosophers need to start thinking like artists or, better still, thinking along with artists. How do we create concepts that productively pass over into sensation(s)? How do we bring concepts to life in a way that affectively resonates, provokes and stays with those who engage our work? What are the appropriate materials, media, aesthetic forms or genre in creating a live event that allows for participation and exper-imentation beyond the contingencies of the moment? How do we avoid the failure of fashioning concepts that simply fall flat and dead on the ground? These, and many others no doubt, will be the kinds of questions that we are provoked to ask and pursue now that we have encountered the Deleuze–Guattarian method of dramatization. And by posing and pursuing questions such as these, the paid-up, state-funded, professional political philosopher can operate within social and political registers that are more conducive to collaborations with artists. For us, it is question of viewing the membrane that separates political practices and aesthetic practices as increasingly porous, of being open to moving through the emerging spaces in which aes-thetic and political practices resonate and connect up. This is indeed a rather rare move for those working within the disciplinary con-fines of political theory. And many a political theorist will no doubt remain to be convinced.

There are, of course, some notable exceptions. For example, there is Simon Critchley's recent collaborative work with the novelist Tom McCarthy under the banner of *The International Necronautical Society (INS)* (Critchley, 2010, 102–122). As 'general secretary' and 'chief phi-losopher' respectively, McCarthy and Critchley collaborated on the INS 'Declaration of Inauthenticity'. This was delivered at an event in Tate Britain, London. The lecturers purporting to be the 'general secretary' and 'chief philosopher', however, were not McCarthy and Critchley, but two actors hired to perform the ideas. The lecture, to put it rather crudely perhaps, became a piece of performance art. Clearly, from the point of view of the method of dramatization, Critchley's collaboration with McCarthy and participation more generally in INS is extremely suggestive in that it forged a set of direct links between philosophy, literature, art and dramatization all bound together by an event. More particularly, it is interesting to note Critchley's rather pointed remarks about how the event at Tate Britain was received within academia, and within academic philosophy in particular. That is to say, when asked by Carl Cederstrom whether they got any response from the 'world of philosophy', Critchley replies: 'resound-ing silence, as is usually the case' (Critchley, 2010, 115). The event did not register at all in philosophical circles; it failed to engage a constituency who presumably view practices such as these as beyond the purview of their concerns.

Critchley's experience in this context brings to mind the very real difficulties and dangers in finding the appropriate materials to use when trying to bring concepts to life and indeed the resistance within academic circles to the intuition that concepts can have a liveness, accessibility and resonance precisely to the extent that they are performed and dramatized. It also, for us, acutely brings into focus the significance of providing a clear ontological or philosophical defence of the method of dramatization such as we mounted earlier in the book (particularly in chapter three). For it is not enough to say that those philosophers who ignore the art-work or aesthetic practices are culturally-politically conservative or parochial in their interests. Their failing is much more dramatic than that. For they fail on philosophical-political grounds; they fail to understand how concepts and the activity of conceptualization, implies a drama that necessarily and inevitably plays through it. Such is the important and resonant provocation of the Deleuze–Guattarian method of dramatization.

Bibliography

Alliez, E. (2004) *The Signature of the World: What is Deleuze and Guattari's Philosophy?* (London: Continuum).

Althusser, L. (1997) *Philosophy and the Spontaneous Philosophy of the Scientists* (London: Verso).

Artaud, A. (1993) *The Theatre and its Double* (London: Calder).

Austin, J. (1975) *How to do Things with Words* (Oxford: Oxford University Press).

Baynes, K. (1992) *The Normative Grounds of Social Criticism: Kant, Rawls and Habermas* (New York: SUNY Press).

Badiou, A. (2009) *Logics of Worlds* (London: Continuum).

Badiou, A. (2005a) *Being and Event* (London: Continuum).

Badiou, A. (2005b) *Handbook of Inaesthetics* (Stanford: Stanford University Press).

Badiou, A. (2004) *Badiou: Theoretical Writings* (London: Continuum).

Badiou, A. (2003) *Infinite Thought: Truth and the Return of Philosophy* (London: Continuum).

Badiou, A. (2000) *Deleuze* (Minneapolis: University of Minnesota Press).

Badiou, A. (1994) 'The Fold, Leibniz and the Baroque', in Boundas, C.V. and Olkowski, D. (eds) *Gilles Deleuze and the Theater of Philosophy* (London: Routledge), pp. 51–69.

Bateson, G. (2000) *Steps to an Ecology of Mind* (Chicago: Chicago University Press).

Bergen, V. (2009) 'Deleuze and the Question of Ontology' in C.V. Boundas (ed.) *Gilles Deleuze: The Intensive Reduction* (London: Continuum), pp. 7–22.

Bergson, H. (2004) *Laughter: An Essay on the Meaning of the Comic* (London: Kessinger Publishing).

Berlin, I. (2002) *Liberty* (Oxford: Oxford University Press).

Boundas, C.V. (ed.) (2009) *Gilles Deleuze: The Intensive Reduction* (Edinburgh: Edinburgh University Press).

Boundas, C.V. and Olkowski, D. (eds) (1994) *Gilles Deleuze and the Theater of Philosophy* (London: Routledge).

Braidotti, R. (2002) *Metamorphoses: Towards a Materialist Theory of Becoming* (Cambridge: Polity).

Brook, P. (2008) *The Empty Space* (London: Penguin).

Buchanan, I. (2008) *Deleuze and Guattari's Anti-Oedipus* (London: Continuum).

Buchanan, I. and Thoburn, N. (eds) (2008) *Deleuze and Politics* (Edinburgh: Edinburgh University Press).

Buchanan, I. and MacCormack, P. (2008) *Deleuze and the Schizoanalysis of Cinema* (London: Continuum).

Colebrook, C. (2006) *Deleuze: A Guide for the Perplexed* (London: Continuum).

Critchley, S. (2010) *How to Stop Living and Start Worrying* (Cambridge: Polity).

Davis, O. (2010) *Jacques Rancière* (Cambridge: Polity).

Deleuze, G. (2006) *Two Regimes of Madness: Texts and Interviews 1975–1995* (Los Angeles: Semiotext(e)).

Deleuze, G. (2004) *Desert Islands and Other Texts 1953–1974* (Los Angeles: Semiotext(e)).
Deleuze, G. (2000) *Proust and Signs* (Minneapolis: University of Minnesota Press).
Deleuze, G. (1995) *Negotiations 1972–1990* (New York: Columbia University Press).
Deleuze, G. (1994) *Difference and Repetition* (New York: Columbia University Press).
Deleuze, G. (1993) *The Fold, Leibniz and the Baroque* (Minneapolis: University of Minnesota Press).
Deleuze, G. (1992) *Cinema 1* (London: Athlone Press).
Deleuze, G. (1991) *Empiricism and Subjectivity: An Essay on Hume's Theory of Human Nature* (New York: Columbia University Press).
Deleuze, G. (1990) *Logic of Sense* (New York: Columbia University Press).
Deleuze, G. (1989) *Cinema 2* (London: Athlone Press).
Deleuze, G. (1988a) *Bergsonism* (New York: Zone Books).
Deleuze, G. (1988b) *Foucault* (Minneapolis: University of Minnesota Press).
Deleuze, G. (1986) *Nietzsche and Philosophy* (London: Athlone Press).
Deleuze, G. (1984) *Kant's Critical Philosophy: The Doctrine of the Faculties* (Minneapolis: University of Minnesota Press).
Deleuze, G. and Guattari, F. (1994) *What is Philosophy?* (London: Verso).
Deleuze, G. and Guattari, F. (1987) *A Thousand Plateaus: Capitalism and Schizophrenia* (Minneapolis: University of Minnesota Press).
Deleuze, G. and Guattari, F. (1986) *Kafka: Towards a Minor Literature* (London: University of Minnesota Press).
Deleuze, G. and Guattari, F. (1977) *Anti-Oedipus: Capitalism and Schizophrenia* (New York: Viking Press).
Deleuze, G. and Parnet, C. (1987) *Dialogues* (London: Athlone Press).
Descartes, R. (2001) *Discourse on Method: Optics, Geometry and Meteorology* (Indianapolis: Hackett Publishing).
Devine, F. (1995) 'Qualitative Analysis' in D. Marsh and G. Stoker (eds) *Theory and Methods in Political Science* (Basingstoke: Macmillan).
Dewesbury, D. and Porter, R. (2010) 'On Broadway', in Dewesbury, D. (ed.) *The Centrifugal Book of Europe* (Belfast: Centrifugal), pp. 34–53.
Evans, B. (2010) 'Life Resistance: Towards a Different Concept of the Political', in M. Svirsky (ed.) *Deleuze Studies: Deleuze and Political Activism*, vol. 4 (supplement), pp. 142–162.
Gadamer, H.G. (1975) *Truth and Method* (London: Sheed and Ward).
Genosko, G. (2002) *Félix Guattari: An Aberrant Introduction* (London: Continuum).
Goodchild, P. (1996) *Deleuze and Guattari: And Introduction to the Politics of Desire* (London: Sage).
Greenberg, C. (1992) 'Modernist Painting', in Frascina, F. and Harris, J. (eds) *Art in Modern Culture* (London: Phaidon), pp. 308–314.
Grosz, E. (2008) *Chaos, Territory, Art: Deleuze and the Framing of the Earth* (New York: Columbia University Press).
Habermas, J. (2000) 'Richard Rorty's Pragmatic Turn', in Brandom, R (ed.) *Rorty and His Critics* (Oxford: Blackwell), pp. 31–55.

Habermas, J. (1990) *Moral Consciousness and Communicative Action* (Cambridge: Polity).

Habermas, J. (1987) *The Philosophical Discourse of Modernity* (Cambridge: Polity).

Habermas, J. (1984) *The Theory of Communicative Action Vol. 1: Reason and the Rationalisation of Society* (Cambridge: Polity).

Habermas, J. (1979) *Communication and the Evolution of Society* (London: Heinemann).

Hardt, M. (1993) *Gilles Deleuze: An Apprenticeship in Philosophy* (Minneapolis: University of Minnesota Press).

Hallward, P. (2006) *Out of this World: Deleuze and the Philosophy of Creation* (London: Verso).

Hallward, P. (2003) *Badiou: A Subject to Truth* (Minneapolis: University of Minnesota Press).

Hayden, P. (1995) 'From Relations to Practice in the Empiricism of Gilles Deleuze', *Man and World*, 28, pp. 283–302.

Hobbes, T. (1968) *Leviathan* (London: Penguin).

Honneth, A. and Joas, H. (eds) (1991) *Communicative Action: Essays on Habermas's The Theory of Communicative Action* (Cambridge: Polity).

Hughes, J. (2009) *Deleuze's Difference and Repetition* (London: Continuum).

Jameson, F. (1991) *Postmodernism: or the Cultural Logic of Late Capitalism* (London: Verso).

Jones, G. and Roffe, R. (eds) (2009) *Deleuze's Philosophical Lineage* (Edinburgh: Edinburgh University Press)

Kant, I. (1952) *The Critique of Judgement* (Oxford: Clarendon Press).

Kaufman, E and Heller, K.J (eds) (1998) *Deleuze and Guattari: New Mappings in Politics, Philosophy and Culture* (Minneapolis: University of Minnesota Press).

Kerslake, C. (2002) 'The Vertigo of Philosophy: Deleuze and the Problem of Immanence', *Radical Philosophy*, 113, pp. 10–23.

Kerslake, C. (2009) *Immanence and the Vertigo of Philosophy: From Kant to Deleuze* (Edinburgh: Edinburgh University Press).

Langley, P. (2007) 'Uncertain Subjects of Anglo-American Financialization', *Cultural Critique*, 65, pp. 67–91.

Lecercle, J.J. (2010) *Badiou and Deleuze Read Literature* (Edinburgh: Edinburgh University Press).

Lecercle, J.J. (2006) *The Marxist Philosophy of Language* (London: Haymarket Books).

Lecercle, J.J. (2002) *Deleuze and Language* (Basingstoke: Palgrave Macmillan).

Lecercle, J.J. (1999a) *Interpretation as Pragmatics* (Basingstoke: Palgrave Macmillan).

Lecercle, J.J. (1999b) 'Cantor, Lacan, Mao, Beckett, *même combat*: The Philosophy of Alain Badiou', *Radical Philosophy*, 93, pp. 6–13.

Lecercle, J.J. (1994) *The Philosophy of Nonsense* (London: Routledge).

Lecercle, J.J. (1990) *The Violence of Language* (London: Routledge).

Lecercle, J.J. (1985) *Philosophy Through the Looking-Glass* (London: Open Court).

MacIntyre, A. (1981) *After Virtue* (London: Duckworth).

MacKenzie, I. (2004) *The Idea of Pure Critique* (London: Continuum).

MacKenzie, I. (2000) 'Beyond the Communicative Turn in Political Philosophy', *Critical Review of International Social and Political Philosophy* 3:4, pp. 1–24.

MacKenzie, I. (1997) 'Creativity as Criticism: The Philosophical Constructivism of Deleuze and Guattari', *Radical Philosophy*, 86, pp. 7–18.

Marsh, D. and Stoker, G. (eds) (1995) *Theory and Methods in Political Science* (Basingstoke: Macmillan).

Marx, K. and Engels, F. *The German Ideology* (London: Penguin).

McCarthy, T. (1978) *The Critical Theory of Jurgen Habermas* (London: Hutchinson).

McLaughlin, G. and Baker, S. (2010) *The Propaganda of Peace* (London: Intellect).

McLellan, D. (2000) *Karl Marx: Selected Writings*, second edition (Oxford: Oxford University Press).

McLuhan, M. (1964) *Understanding Media* (London: Routledge).

McMahon, M. (2009) 'Immanuel Kant' in Jones, G. and Roffe, R. (eds) *Deleuze's Philosophical Lineage* (Edinburgh: Edinburgh University Press), pp. 87–103.

O'Neill, S. (1997) *Impartiality in Context: Grounding Justice in a Pluralist World* (New York: SUNY Press).

Pappas, N. (2003) *Plato and The Republic* (London: Routledge).

Patton, P. (2010) *Deleuzean Concepts: Philosophy, Colonization, Politics* (Stanford: Stanford University Press).

Patton, P (2007) 'Utopian Political Philosophy: Deleuze and Rawls,' *Deleuze Studies*, 1:1, pp. 41–59.

Patton, P. (2005) 'Deleuze and Democratic Politics' in Tønder, L. and Thomassen L. (eds) *Radical Democracy: Politics between Abundance and Lack* (Manchester: Manchester University Press), pp. 50–67.

Patton, P. (2000) *Deleuze and the Political* (London: Routledge).

Porter, R. (2010) 'From Clichés to Slogans: Towards a Deleuze–Guattarian Critique of Ideology', *Social Semiotics*, 20:3, pp. 233–245.

Porter, R. (2009) *Deleuze and Guattari: Aesthetics and Politics* (Cardiff: University of Wales Press).

Porter, R. (2007) 'Habermas in Pleasantville', *Contemporary Political Theory*, 6:4, pp. 405–418.

Porter, R. (2006) *Ideology: Contemporary Social, Political and Cultural Theory* (Cardiff: University of Wales Press).

Protevi, J. and Patton, P. (2003) *between Derrida and Deleuze* (London: Continuum).

Rancière, J. (2009) *The Emancipated Spectator* (London: Verso).

Rancière, J. (2007) *The Future of the Image* (London: Verso).

Rancière, J. (2006) *Film Fables* (Oxford: Berg).

Rancière, J. (2004) *The Politics of Aesthetics: The Distribution of the Sensible* (London: Continuum).

Rancière, J. (2004) 'Aesthetics, Inaesthetics, Anti-Aesthetics', in Hallward, P. (ed.) *Think Again: Alain Badiou and the Future of Philosophy* (London: Continuum), pp. 218–31.

Rancière, J. (2003) *The Philosopher and his Poor* (Durham: Duke University Press).

Rancière, J. (1991) *The Ignorant Schoolmaster* (Stanford: Stanford University Press).

Rancière, J. (1989) *The Nights of Labour* (Philadelphia: Temple University Press).

Read, J. (2003) *The Micro-Politics of Capital: Marx and the Prehistory of the Present* (New York: SUNY Press).

Rèe, J. (1995) 'Philosophy for Philosophy's Sake', *New Left Review*, 211, pp. 105–11.

Ricoeur, P. (1981) *Hermeneutics and the Human Sciences: Essays on Language, Action and Interpretation* (Cambridge: Cambridge University Press).

Rodowick, D. (1997) *Gilles Deleuze's Time Machine* (Durham: Duke University Press).

Rorty, R. (2000) 'Universality and Truth' in Brandom, R (ed.) *Rorty and His Critics* (Oxford: Blackwell), pp. 1–30.

Shapiro, M.J. (2002) 'Genres, Technologies and Spaces of Being-in-Common', in Finlayson, A. and Valentine, J. (eds) *Politics and Poststructuralism* (Edinburgh: Edinburgh University Press), pp. 206–22.

Shapiro, M.J. (1999) *Cinematic Political Thought: Narrating Race, Nation and Gender* (Edinburgh: Edinburgh University Press).

Shirlow, P. and Murtagh, B. (2006) *Belfast* (London: Pluto).

Skinner, Q. (2008) *Hobbes and Republican Liberty* (Cambridge: Cambridge University Press).

Smith, D. (2006) 'Deleuze, Kant and the Theory of Immanent Ideas', in Boundas (ed.) *Deleuze and Philosophy* (Edinburgh: Edinburgh University Press) pp. 43–61.

Smith, D. (2003) 'Mathematics and the Theory of Multiplicities: Badiou and Deleuze Revisited', *Southern Journal of Philosophy*, 41:3, pp. 411–449.

Stivale, C. (1998) *The Two-Fold Thought of Deleuze and Guattari: Intersections and Animations* (New York: The Guildford Press).

Svirsky, M. (ed.) (2010) *Deleuze Studies: Deleuze and Political Activism*, vol. 4, supplement, (Edinburgh: Edinburgh University Press).

Taylor, C. (1989) *Sources of the Self* (Cambridge: Cambridge University Press).

Taylor, C. (1985a) *Philosophy and the Human Sciences* (Cambridge: Cambridge University Press).

Taylor, C. (1985b) *Human Agency and Language* (Cambridge: Cambridge University Press).

Thoburn, N. (2003) *Deleuze, Marx, Politics* (London: Routledge).

Toscano, A. (2009) 'Gilbert Simondon' in G. Jones and J. Roffe (eds) *Deleuze's Philosophical Lineage* (Edinburgh: Edinburgh University Press), pp 380–99.

Tully, J. (1995) *Strange Multiplicity: Constitutionalism in an Age of Diversity* (Cambridge: Cambridge University Press).

Widder, N. (2001) 'The Rights of Simulacra: Deleuze and the Univocity of Being', *Continental Philosophy Review*, 34, pp. 437–453.

Williams, J. (2009) 'If not here, then where? On the Location and Individuation of Events in Deleuze and Badiou', *Deleuze Studies*, 3:1, pp. 97–123.

Williams, J. (2008) *Gilles Deleuze's Logic of Sense: A Critical Introduction and Guide* (Edinburgh: Edinburgh University Press).

Williams, J. (2003) *Gilles Deleuze's Difference and Repetition: A Critical Introduction and Guide* (Edinburgh: Edinburgh University Press).

Žižek, S. (2004) *Organs Without Bodies: Deleuze and Consequences* (London: Routledge).

Index